Celebrating the Christian Year

Alan Griffiths is a priest of the Roman Catholic Diocese of Portsmouth. He studied Liturgy at the Pontifical Liturgical Academy of Sant' Anselmo in Rome and taught liturgical studies at Saint John's Seminary, Wonersh, from 1977 to 1983. He was a member of the panel that produced *Opening Prayers, Scripture-related Collects for Years A, B and C from the Sacramentary* (Canterbury Press, 1999) and has translated the Ambrosian Eucharistic Prefaces, published as *We Give You Thanks and Praise* (Canterbury Press, 1999). He has worked as a drafter and editor of texts for a National Proper collection commissioned by the Roman Catholic Bishops Conference of England and Wales. He works currently as a liturgical consultant active in the field of Church building and renovation.

Celebrating the Christian Year

Prayers and Resources for Sundays, Holy
Days and Festivals – Years A, B and C

Volume III: Advent and the Christmas Season

Compiled by Alan Griffiths

CANTERBURY
PRESS
Norwich

© in this compilation Alan Griffiths 2005

First published in 2005 by the Canterbury Press Norwich
(a publishing imprint of Hymns Ancient & Modern Limited,
a registered charity)
St Mary's Works, St Mary's Plain,
Norwich, Norfolk, NR3 3BH

www.scm-canterburypress.co.uk

British Library Cataloguing in Publication data

A catalogue record for this book is available
from the British Library

ISBN 1-85311-671-8/9781-85311-671-1

Typeset by Regent Typesetting, London
Printed and bound in Great Britain by
William Clowes Ltd, Beccles, Suffolk

CONTENTS

INTRODUCTION

Volume III of *Celebrating the Christian Year* is a collection of texts and service outlines designed for use during the 'Christmas Cycle' of the Church's Year, which runs from Advent Sunday through to the celebration of the Baptism of Christ.

Like the first volume, this collection follows the course of the Lectionary as set out in *Common Worship*. I hope this will render it usable not only in Anglican congregations, but also in other church communities that use the *Revised Common Lectionary*, which is very close to that of *Common Worship*. The Roman Catholic Lectionary too is similar, indeed historically it is the inspiration for the other two. So I hope that Roman Catholic communities also might find themselves able to make use of some of these texts. Roman Catholics will find here many prayers that will be familiar to them from the Roman Missal, though in fresh translations.

This is a resource collection and not a complete service book. It does not normally include outlines or texts for main services, or (with the exception of the Eucharistic Prayer) texts that are repeatedly used, such as those for the Intercession. These differ between traditions, denominations and churches. I hope people will make use of the texts contained here in whatever way they find appropriate.

As in the previous two volumes, I have tried to maintain a liturgical style that echoes the English styles currently used in most of the major denominations. As in all liturgical books, some of the prayers will require reading beforehand as preparation on the part of those who speak them. I have tried to make them as uncomplicated as I can, however.

Overview of Advent, Christmas and Epiphany

After the Easter Festival, with its fifty days of paschal celebration culminating in the feast of Pentecost, the second most important season of the Christian Year is that of Christmas and Epiphany, which runs from the first Sunday of Advent until the celebration of the Baptism of Christ in early January.

It would only be mildly ironic to recall that in our secularized society 'The Festive Season' lasts (more or less) from late November until 25 December. Then follows a season of retreat in order to recover from it all until the arrival of the next great party season at the New Year on 31 December/1 January. The publicly acknowledged Christian content of this season seems to be diminishing year by year and in many places is actively discouraged. Christian believers of all traditions can sense a widening gulf between the secular Christmas and the religious celebration. This sense of difference is likely to increase even more in the future.

This is not necessarily a bad thing. Perhaps the sense of growing divergence will move Christian believers to reclaim something of the real shape and character of their celebration of the coming of Jesus Christ. They will then have a good chance of experiencing more deeply how their celebration differs both in its character and in its extent from the secular Christmas.

It is important to begin this process of reclamation by recovering the sense that Advent, Christmas and Epiphany constitute one unfolding cycle of celebration and serve one single theological narrative. An examination of the lectionaries introduced in the last forty years or so in the major churches will reveal that this approach has indeed emerged.

The Lectionary and texts of *Common Worship* have in fact taken the seasonal approach to Advent/Christmas/Epiphany one stage further than earlier lectionaries. *Common Worship* envisages the Christmas Season extending throughout January and only ending on 2 February, with the festival commonly known as 'Candlemas'. This feast commemorates the visit of Joseph and Mary to the Temple to 'present' their child to the

Lord. In fact, this is not a recent invention but a return to a more ancient tradition. For in earlier times Christmas was held to continue beyond 'Twelfth Night' and only to be completed by the commemoration of the Presentation of Christ in the Temple and the announcement of his mission and destiny by the prophet Simeon. Other traditions of popular devotion retain Christmas and Epiphany themes in church throughout the early New Year. In Italy, for example, it is common for parishes to keep their elaborate Christmas Crib in place well beyond Epiphany, often leaving it in place until the beginning of Lent.

The history of the Christmas season, insofar as it is possible to know it, is interesting and will help to explain its shape. It is understandable to think that Christmas has always been there, as part of the Christian 'thing' from the very beginning. This is not the case, however. Strange though it might seem, the evidence suggests that a celebration of Christmas only evolved after some three centuries of Christian history. From the very beginning, all the churches appear to have kept Sunday as their weekly holy day, the 'Day of the Lord' in honour of the risen Christ. Easter, the annual 'Passover', seems to have emerged very early across the Christian world. But it seems that Christians got on quite well for over three hundred years without a historical commemoration of Jesus' birthday. However, from the fourth century of the Christian Era, evidence begins to appear of such a festival.

Though its exact nature and origin are open to debate, it seems that a cycle of feasts based on either the birth of Jesus or his 'appearing' (in Greek *epiphaneia*) as Son of God was beginning to develop by the beginning of the fourth century. What is significant for the development of the Christmas cycle is that soon after this time, Imperial recognition began to be given to the Christian Church. Thus the faith of the martyrs was able to emerge from the shadows as an increasingly important part of the public life of the Roman Empire and its great Persian neighbour.

This dramatic change in status for the Christian faith was accompanied by a sharp rise in the theological temperature.

Freed from external persecution, Christians had time for their own theological disagreements. The age of the great debates and Ecumenical Councils in Christianity began. In concert with the Roman State, now highly receptive to the Christian faith, the Churches engaged in vigorous and sometimes violent dispute about the person and nature of Jesus, that is to say, *who* Jesus was and *what* Jesus was. Between the beginning of the fourth century and the last years of the fifth, these questions occupied the intellect and the lyrical skills of the greatest Church leaders, theologians and liturgical composers.

Such was the context in which the events surrounding the birth and appearing of Jesus first became the subject of a developing liturgical cycle. Worship and belief went hand in hand. The adage 'Let the rule of prayer establish the rule of belief' was never more truly spoken than at this time. To celebrate Jesus' birth, or the commencement of his public ministry, was to make a statement about faith in his divinity. It is this coupling of narrative and dogmatic assertion that gives us the origin, both historically and theologically, of the Christmas and Epiphany cycle.

It is possible that the feast of Epiphany is the oldest part of the Christmas cycle. Certainly it is the richest. In most ancient Christian traditions, it is the feast of Epiphany that draws out the full meaning of the Incarnation of the Son of God. While Anglicans and others are accustomed to thinking of Epiphany as commemorating the coming of the Magi, most other Christian traditions see Epiphany as primarily the feast of Jesus' Baptism, at which he was revealed as the 'beloved Son' in what is usually seen as a Trinitarian revelation. The Father announces the Son and the Spirit is sent from the Father to anoint him as the Christ. It is the Baptism that announces his mission as the Servant of the Lord. The Orthodox churches still echo the baptismal theme of this festival by blessing water. Modern calendars and lectionaries have drawn on all these traditions to provide a celebration of Epiphany and the Lord's Baptism, as well as the sign of Cana-in-Galilee, where 'he showed his glory' (John 2:11).

In both Catholic and Reformed traditions, the concentration on Jesus' nativity as 'the' Christmas event has meant that we have lost this wider and more authentic view. Translated to the secular culture, this has meant that the nativity of Jesus is remembered simply as an archetypal human birth, without its deeper, salvific significance. Indeed, in the secular world, the sentimentalized 'nativity scene' has quite obscured the Christian meaning of the event. In its turn, such a de-Christianized view has itself given way to the even vaguer images of 'Santa Claus' and the politically correct 'Season's Greetings'. Peace and good-will may still be invoked, but neither the angels who first pro-claimed it nor the momentous event that inspired their message has been remembered. Christmas, thank goodness, still remains a festival for families and children in particular. But it is hard to see how this will survive without the profoundly religious core that gave it meaning.

All this makes it more important than ever for Christians to hold on to the fact that the celebration of Advent and the festivals of Epiphany and Christ's Baptism are both essential for an understanding and proper celebration of his birth. For those who plan and lead worship, a frequent problem is that secular institutions frequently insist on Christmas carol services long before 25 December. Even more frustrating is the assumption in many congregations that once November is over it is necessary to start singing Christmas carols at services. While sensitive and selective use of such material may indeed find a place in Advent – with some support in existing liturgical traditions – it remains true that the 'Away in a manger' theme sits uneasily with the messages of Advent.

Christmas is not just about the human birth of Jesus. More significant is its revelation that here is God himself made mani-fest in our time and place, the eternal Word made Flesh. The meaning of Christmas is expressed in the 'waiting time' of Advent. The meaning of this holy birth is likewise made known in the stories and feasts that follow Christmas itself: the martyr Stephen, John the Evangelist, the Innocents, the Magi and their gifts, the descent of the Spirit at the Jordan, the mysterious wine not made by human hands for the Cana wedding. Why should this be so?

Introduction

The traditional readings for the Eucharist of Christmas Day provide the best clue to the significance of Christmas and to why the whole season has developed as it has. This selection, from the opening of the Letter to the Hebrews and the Prologue to Saint John's Gospel, was from an early date the principal set of readings for Christmas Day in the Roman Rite. *The Book of Common Prayer*, itself derived from the Roman Rite through the Sarum Use, reproduced this selection.

At first glance, it might seem strange that neither of these Eucharistic readings makes any detailed mention of the birth of Jesus such as is present in the Gospels of Matthew and Luke. While most people nowadays would regard reference to the Birth narratives as essential at Christmas, in the Roman tradition it is only in the other two lesser Mass formularies, those for the 'midnight' and 'dawn' masses, that the narrative from Luke is employed. Clearly the primary interest of this tradition lies not in the manger, but elsewhere.

Christmas developed as a feast encompassing the whole meaning of Christ, a reflection of emerging Christian dogmatic teaching. The founding theme of Christmas and Epiphany is that the eternal Word, the co-eternal Son, equal to the Father, appeared in the world, incarnate and born as one of the human race, so that humankind might be reborn and made a partaker in the Divine Nature. On the deepest level, Christmas is not in fact centred on the birth of a child, but on the coming of an adult Christ.

It is noteworthy that many of the best Christmas carols and hymns offer this same vision of redemption as implicit in the birth of Jesus. At the conclusion of the great Christmas hymn 'Hark! The herald angels sing' these lines are sung:

Mild, he lays his glory by,
Born that man no more may die,
Born to raise the sons of earth,
Born to give them second birth.

They are of course familiar. Less so is the final verse, now restored in the *New English Hymnal*. It includes these lines, which develop the theme of a theology of redemption. Address-ing the newborn Son, the text reads:

Now display thy saving power,
Ruined nature now restore,
Now in mystic union join
Thine to ours and ours to thine.

The restoration of creation, the new birth of humankind, the making divine of what is human, are all themes implicit in the celebration of Christmas. However, it will be immediately recognized that these are in the first place *Easter* themes. It will be clear from the hymn quoted above, and from many of the texts contained in this collection, that Christmas claims a paschal significance.

This is true in two ways. First, Christmas, like Easter, is a celebration of new birth and new light. The human birth of the Incarnate Word was the prelude to the new birth offered to believers in baptism. The waters that are both tomb and womb give birth to a new people, incorporated in the dying and rising of Christ, the 'Firstborn from the dead'. Christmas is, as it were, an Easter in winter. The Light associated with the celebration of the Easter event also figures greatly in the scriptural and prayer texts associated with the Christmas season.

Second, both the Easter and the Christmas narrative imply the return of Christ in glory. Saint Luke's account of the Ascension of Christ (Acts 1:11) has the angels telling the Apostles *This Jesus, who has been taken up from you into heaven, will come in the same way as you saw him go into heaven.* This aspect of Christmas is partly responsible for the creation of the season of Advent, which focuses both on the expectation of Christ's first coming in his human birth and, by association, on the Second Coming of Christ. Associated with this theme is a focus on 'the Last Things' and the ministry of those, such as Isaiah and John the Baptist, who have prepared 'the way of the Lord'.

So the creation of the Advent/Christmas/Epiphany cycle of celebration derives from the central narrative of the Christian gospel, the Paschal Mystery of the dying and rising and glorification of the Christ. It explores the deepest meaning of the Christmas event by revealing its paschal and eschatological character.

In this respect, it is strikingly similar to what we know of the character and development of the tradition established in the Gospels. The Gospel of Saint Mark, commonly held to be the earliest of the Gospels in their present form, begins with the Baptism of Jesus and his revelation there as the Christ of God. By his words *The beginning of the good news of Jesus Christ, the Son of God* (Mark 1:1), Saint Mark establishes the principle that right at the beginning of the Gospel narrative the true nature of Jesus of Nazareth should be announced. Saint Matthew and Saint Luke continue this tradition, but, for their announcement of the Messiah, they go back beyond the baptism to the birth and the events preceding it. The purpose of the infancy narratives that they created is that of the Gospel as a whole, the announcing of Jesus as the Christ. They weave a wonderful and mysterious story that is quite unlike anything else in their Gospel account. They do this by the creative employment of ancient prophetic and other texts. The American biblical scholar Raymond Brown has shown in great detail how both Matthew and Luke employ the texts of the Old Testament to create their stories of Joseph's calling, the Annunciation to Zechariah and to Mary, the Birth of Jesus, the Magi and Herod.

Such scholarly investigations shed an intriguing light on the choice of readings in both ancient and modern lectionaries for Advent and Christmas. Often, the same texts used or referred to by the evangelists are used in the liturgies of those seasons. To take one slightly less well-known example, the daily Roman Lectionary for the second half of Advent includes the narrative of Balaam and Balak from Leviticus 24:17. Balak calls on the seer Balaam to curse the Israelites encamped on his borders and posing a threat to his security. Balaam obliges, but not with curses. He speaks instead of the greatness of this new people. He speaks too of the 'star' which 'arises from Jacob' and which 'takes the leadership' over the nations. We need look no further than that for the 'Star in the East' of Matthew 2:2, 9.

Christmas, then, is like a window. It opens out on to the visionary horizon of Easter, the cosmic significance of the Risen Christ who is to come again as we have seen him go. In order for this Christian vision to be fully appreciated, the Church's worship tradition has evolved in winter a seasonal sequence modelled on Easter and its 'last and greatest day' and feast of mission, Pentecost. In this scheme, Advent is the time of preparation (originally reflecting Lent) and Christmas/Epiphany the season of subsequent rejoicing. The Baptism of Jesus, a feast of mission, concludes the season.

The Content of this Book

This book contains material for optional use in the Eucharist, main service or other services on the Sundays and festivals of Advent and Christmas until the Baptism of Christ. The prayers are arranged as follows:

- As in the preceding two volumes, an opening prayer is given for each of the three years A, B and C of the *Common Worship* Lectionary cycle. This **Scripture-related opening prayer** takes its inspiration from the readings for the day in question. My hope has been that these prayers will serve for those who want to base their prayer in the Word of God. This opening prayer may be used as a collect, or at other times in the service. Some preachers have employed these texts as short prayer meditations after a sermon or homily, or used them during the silence after Communion. They may find a variety of uses. I have laid out these prayers in paragraphs, as in the previous volume, to help those who speak them.
- A collect or **opening prayer** is given. This offers a further choice at this point. I have drawn many of these prayers from the newly revised edition of the Roman Missal and also from the Ambrosian Missal of the Church of Milan. In each case the translation is my own.
- Verses for the **Acclamation** before the Gospel are also suggested, to be sung with the refrain 'Alleluia' as set out

frequently in the text. A full description of how to perform this acclamation may be found in Volume I of this series on p. xiii.

- A third collect is given which may be used to conclude the **Intercession**. This third collect is often cast as a prayer for the Church, or with a mission theme, making it suitable for use at this point.
- When the bread and wine are 'taken' by the president at the Table, a short prayer, the **Prayer over the Gifts,** is often said before the beginning of the Eucharistic Prayer. I have included a large and seasonally related collection of these texts, since the original provision in *Common Worship* was not large and many of the prayers seemed to lack any real relationship to the season. The prayers in this collection focus sometimes on the thanksgiving about to be offered, or on the fellowship to which Christ calls his people at his table.
- A **Eucharistic Preface** to begin the Eucharistic Prayer is also given. The prefaces express the great thematic richness of the Advent and Christmas season. Many of them are theological lyrics, sometimes of great beauty.
- After the sharing of the Sacrament, a variable prayer is often said before the blessing. The **Prayers after Communion** in this collection refer usually to the gifts that have been received in the context of the liturgical season or festival. However, in line with the function of such prayers both to conclude part of the rite and to begin another part, the texts often refer to the mission of the Church, which awaits it as a direct result of sharing the Eucharist.

For the principal Saints' days during this season, a similar collection of prayers is offered, though I have not always included a Scripture-related opening prayer.

In addition to the texts for regular services, I have followed the other volumes by including outlines and other material for special seasonal services. Advent and Christmas offer great opportunities for such acts of worship, whose outreach is often far greater than that of the regular worship.

In line with Volume II, I have included a specimen of a Eucharistic Prayer. Including this is probably no more than an experiment, since this element of the Eucharist is probably the most 'controlled' of all the prayer texts in every tradition and so most users of this book may not feel able legitimately to use it. However, it is reasonable to ask, in a history of the Eucharistic Prayer that is still unfolding, how that prayer might more flexibly adapt to reflect the season. I have based this text on a prayer shape common in the ancient Spanish Mass, usually known as the Mozarabic Rite, which the Catholic Church in Spain has recently revived, and for which it has now prepared a new Missal and Lectionary.

Some Details: The Conclusion of Collects

Collects usually end with an acknowledgement that prayer is made to the Father through Jesus Christ. In this collection, I have used the traditional short ending: '(We make this prayer/we ask this) through Jesus Christ our Lord.' For a more 'solemn' ending, often employed with the opening Collect, the Trinitarian relationships are invoked in something like this form:

> *Through Jesus Christ your Son,*
> *who is one with you and the Holy Spirit,*
> *now and for ever.*

This echoes, with less elaboration, the traditional ending found in *Common Worship* collects.

Such endings may be used with most of the collects in this book. I have tried to vary the endings, partly to allow for those who prefer to avoid terms such as 'Lord' and 'reigns', partly to allow for variety. Those who prefer to use the more traditional endings will find that they are usable with most of the collects given in the body of the text.

The Beginning and Ending of the Prefaces

Traditionally, the first line of the preface echoes the congregational response: 'It is right to give thanks and praise' – 'It is truly right . . .'.

I have usually kept to this traditional opening for the prefaces in this book, employing forms such as this:

It is truly right and just, our duty and our salvation,
always and everywhere to give you thanks,
Lord, holy Father, almighty and eternal God,
(through Jesus Christ our Lord).

The variant preface opening most often used in this book resembles the traditional opening by echoing an earlier line of the dialogue between president and congregation: 'Lift up your hearts.' It begins something like this:

We lift up our hearts to you,
God eternal, true and faithful;
to you we offer thanks and praise
through Jesus Christ your Son.

Preface openings are usually interchangeable, so if this form is preferred, it can be used with most of the prefaces in this book.

The preface ending also varies. The traditional ending names the various ranks of heavenly beings, angels, archangels, thrones, dominions, powers and so on. In older liturgical books, these endings were sometimes very elaborate and reflected contemporary interest in the orders and degrees of angelic beings:

And so, with angels and archangels,
thrones and dominions,
and with all the powers of heaven,
we glorify your holy name
in this, their ageless hymn of praise:

The Prayer Book simplified this somewhat, and subsequent English prefaces have maintained its reference to a less complicated heavenly hierarchy.

However, there are other, shorter, forms, such as

And so, with angels and saints,
we glorify your holy name:

These preface endings are often interchangeable. The dynamic of the liturgy demands, however, that the congregation is cued to enter with 'Holy, Holy . . .'.

The Collection as a Whole

This collection completes a work that the Canterbury Press encouraged me to begin some four years ago. In retrospect, it was an ambitious project to prepare such a collection of liturgical prayers and other material for the whole Christian Year. I certainly did not realize the amount of work that would be involved but neither did I underestimate the satisfaction I would derive from it. Two aspects in particular have been most challenging.

First there was the preparation of so many original texts for the Scripture-related opening prayers. This involved not merely knowing thoroughly the Lectionary provision for any given occasion, but carefully evaluating its themes and imagery so as to decide what might offer the best opportunities for the creation of a prayer. I know from past experience that such an account of the process sounds much more organized than in fact it is. Inspiration plays the greater part, so I hope users of these texts will forgive my sometimes having created prayers that are a touch too obviously related to one or other scriptural text, or indeed texts whose relation to a set of readings may be somewhat unclear.

Second, there was the translation of many texts from older sources, often the ancient sacramentaries of the Roman and other traditions. Readers will be aware that the issue of what constitutes fitting translation for liturgical use is a hotly disputed question in many church circles at the present time. I wrote in Volume I of this series that I had attempted to find a style that allows the insights of the ancient texts to speak in a way that is neither so informal as to lose the nuances of the original, nor so complex as to obscure the expression of those insights. Over many years, I have found that early texts treat the story of salvation in a refreshingly humane and sacramental way. We seem to be in the midst of a theological revolution in which both the accepted medieval accounts of the Atonement are being re-evaluated and a fresher, more ritually focused account of the Christian sacraments is emerging. Ancient liturgical texts predate the emergence of much abstract (and divisive) medieval theology and are ready to be rediscovered as sources and companions for that new approach.

Over the last few years, I have had a great deal of help with these volumes. I want to thank in particular Christine Smith and Mary Matthews of SCM-Canterbury Press for the help and support they have offered in matters both theoretical and technical as well as for the initial inspiration for the three volumes. I have also many friends to thank who listened to texts both new and old to see how they sounded, corrected mistakes and improved the flow. I feel very grateful also to the many other authors who have kindly allowed me to use their work.

In the ninth century, the Emperor Charlemagne decided that the churches in his empire should have but one liturgy and that should be the Roman one. He called for the Pope to send him the books. Unfortunately, the books were incomplete. Someone had to prepare a set of liturgical resources to enable the book to cover the whole Christian Year. These were put together, possibly by the great English monk and scholar Alcuin of York, more likely by one Benedict of Aniane.

A document called the *Praefatiuncula Hucusque* ('Little Preface to Part Two') accompanied this collection, which eventually became the basis for the medieval missals of the churches in communion with the See of Rome.

The book was divided in two with the *Praefatiuncula* in the middle. Part One was the series of texts used by the Pope. This collection, the preface stated, should be regarded as compulsory. The second part should, it modestly declared, be for optional use. If these texts *in animo sedent* – 'lodge in the soul' – then let them be used.

I hope that some at least of the texts in this series will lodge in the soul of those who use them.

Alan Griffiths
Advent 2004

PART ONE

PROPER TEXTS FOR
THE SUNDAYS OF ADVENT

The Season of Advent – Beginning or Ending?

The season of Advent marks the beginning of the Christian Year, the Church's calendar of liturgical celebration. The word 'Advent' comes from the Latin for 'coming' and so the season is about Christ's coming among us. But what is intended by 'coming'?

At first sight, the content of the term 'the coming' of Christ would seem to be a simple matter. It is tempting to think that the beginning of the Church's calendar ought to be about the beginnings of Jesus. The Christian Year surely ought to start with the Christmas story. However, it is not that straightforward and a glance at the Lectionary or any prayer book will reveal something quite different. On the opening Sunday of Advent in all three years of the cycle the Scripture readings seem to be speaking of ends, not beginnings. The season announces itself with the fanfare of apocalypse:

> . . . the sun will be darkened
> and the moon will not give its light,
> and the stars will be falling from heaven
> and the powers in the heavens shall be shaken.
> Then they will see 'the Son of Man coming in clouds . . .'
> *(Mark 13:24–26)*

The hymn 'Lo! He comes with clouds descending!' and many other similar songs are popular during Advent. Charles Wesley's text is majestic in its imagery:

Thousand thousand saints attending,
Swell the triumph of his train;
Alleluia! Alleluia!
God appears, on earth to reign.

Every eye shall now behold him
Robed in dreadful majesty . . .

This awesome proclamation of the return of Christ in judgement, the bliss of the just and the discomfiture of the unrighteous, resounds with the sense of impending catastrophe. It looks more as if the Christian Year is beginning with the end, the 'Last Things'. Is it, in fact, looking more to the Day of Judgement than to the manger at Bethlehem?

To solve this apparent contradiction one must look at the weeks immediately preceding Advent in the Church's calendar, since it is with these that the opening themes of Advent have much in common. The Sunday readings for the later Sundays of November also tell the story of 'the end time'. This has become more marked in recent years, as the Sunday Lectionary has developed to take the period between the Festival of All Saints and the beginning of Advent as a special season focusing on 'the Kingdom' in all its aspects.

From the beginning of November, we are urged to think of 'the Last Things'. The day following All Saints is observed as 'All Souls' Day', a day of remembering our Christian dead. The Sunday Scripture readings draw on the prophecies of universal collapse in the apocalyptic literature of the later Jewish scriptures and parallel these with the apocalyptic sayings of Jesus that precede the narrative of the passion in the Synoptic Gospels.

As the leaves fall, the climate cools and the nights draw in (at least in the northern hemisphere), perhaps it is not surprising that 'endings' and eschatology have become a popular theme. Additionally, in British national life, the month of November brings us Remembrance Sunday with its various commemorations of those who died in wartime.

In the popular religious culture of nearly all Roman Catholic countries, the month of November is dedicated to prayer for the faithful departed. Parishes organize visits to their cemetery, and people are encouraged to pray daily for their dead. In this tradition, it is clear that the faithful departed are still members of the Body of Christ, and therefore cannot be excluded from the Eucharist or from the earthly prayer of the Church.

There is a great deal of evidence that in the British Isles before the Reformation people were very concerned to express their feeling for the dead in prayer and worship. However, the years of religious change comprehensively deleted this tradition. The reformers rejected prayer for the dead. God had eternally decreed the destiny of the righteous and sinners, so prayer after death was not merely irrelevant but presumptious. The effects of this have outlived the Reformation and persisted even into our own time.

The shift in thinking meant primarily that the dead suffered excommunication. The faithful departed came to be viewed no longer as fellow members of the Church who sleep in Christ, but rather as aliens, ghostly visitants and beings to be feared. The departed gradually became excluded from the active memory and work of the Church.

This may partly account for the fact of the transposition of All Saints' Eve into 'Hallowe'en'. What should be a confident prayer to the God of salvation for the repose of departed souls has been corrupted into a preoccupation with the unearthly dead. Later on this too has been supplanted by the commercialized trivia of 'spooks' and 'things that go bump in the night'. Many Christians are concerned that this is a sign of a resurgent paganism. This may or may not be the case. What is clear is that it seems to signal a thoroughly unchristian attitude to 'the Last Things' and the faithful departed. It certainly militates against the perfectly natural and Christian desire to pray that those we have lost may, in the words of one of our most ancient eucharistic prayers, be accorded a 'place of consolation, light and peace'.

Maybe the autumnal sense of the ending of things is a survival of something much older than Christianity. Ancient peoples feared the onset of winter and the echoes of such apprehension may still be heard. Acting on the conviction that 'Grace builds on Nature' and does not overturn it, the Church attempted to make some of these older rituals Christian, so as to change the world-view that accompanied them.

So it is that the 'Kingdom Season' and then Advent speak of the ultimate realities, in particular the 'coming of the Son of Man' as Judge. Traditional reaction to this has been fearful and apprehensive in 'Prepare to meet thy God' mode. Though under-standable, this may not be the only way of looking at 'the Last Things'. It is true that the scriptures use the language of universal catastrophe and collapse, but that imagery hides a much more positive message about the purposes of God for human beings and for the whole creation. Fundamental to this message is the ambivalence of 'judgement'. It is as well to remember that it is a term carrying several meanings. It implies not simply the forensic ideas of verdict and sentence but also the social and ethical themes of justice and the human qualities of maturity, common sense and discernment that are required for both.

The prophet Isaiah features prominently in Advent. His call is precisely a call for justice; his vision is that of the One who will bring justice and its companion, peace, to all nations. It is important to remember that we can translate the words of the Creed: *He will come again in glory to judge the living and the dead* in another way and say, with equal scriptural correctness but quite different emphasis: *He will come again in glory to do justice for the living and the dead.* While we are inclined to think of 'judgement' in an individualistic way, it is also necessary to think of it in terms of putting things to rights in the public domain. Isaiah called for precisely this:

> Wash yourselves, make yourselves clean;
> remove the evil of your doings from before my eyes;
> cease to do evil, learn to do good:
> seek justice, rescue the oppressed,
> defend the orphan, plead for the widow.
> *(Isaiah 1:17)*

Judgement and justice are both Advent themes, though in our Lectionaries the second has rather greater prominence than the first. This is where John the Baptist is so significant. The figure of John is crucial to Advent. John's story is told on no less than two out of its four Sundays. Biblical scholars debate the relationship of John to Jesus. Whatever the truth about this was, the Gospels portray John's ministry as that of the 'Forerunner' of Christ. John is an apocalyptic figure himself, calling the people to repentance before the final, fiery judgement comes. However, John insists that such repentance must take the form of deeds of justice.

But John is also portrayed as the messianic herald of Jesus of Nazareth. Indeed in Saint Luke's Gospel John and Jesus are kindred. So John is as intimately concerned with the Birth of Jesus as he is with the revelation of Jesus as the 'One who is to come'. In this way, John the Baptist acts as the bridge between the Old and New Testaments, the 'hinge' on which Advent turns.

The season of Advent, in fact, has a twofold focus. The focus on the 'coming' of Christ is both on his coming at the end of time and on his human birth. These two themes are interwoven in Advent. It is a season of waiting and vigil, the time of the brides-maids waiting for the Bridegroom, the great figures of the Old Testament waiting for the Messiah, John the Baptist waiting at the Jordan river and the young girl, Mary, laden with the angel's awesome promise, awaiting the birth of the child in her womb, the child who is both Son of Man and Son of God. Advent draws out all these facets of the 'coming' of Jesus, so as to reveal its nature as anticipation of the fullness of the Christmas event.

For about the first half of the season, the more universal element predominates. With the story of John, the season turns more specifically towards the events surrounding the Birth of Christ. The Fourth Sunday, for example, is almost a festival of Mary, the God-Bearer. The daily eucharistic Lectionary for the eight days from 17 December to Christmas Eve uses the first chapter of Saint Luke's Gospel, telling the story of John's Annunciation and birth, and then the parallel story of the Annunciation of the Christ to Mary.

5

Historically, Advent seems to be a season that grew up in the Latin-speaking churches of the West. In early medieval Rome, Advent eventually developed into a four-week season. In Milan, Advent is still six weeks in length. Traditionally, it has been viewed as a penitential season similar to Lent. Vestments of a darker colour, blue or violet, are worn. More recently, however, its penitential character has been less emphasized. The revised General Calendar of the Roman Catholic Church hits exactly the right note when it describes Advent as 'a season of joyful and spiritual expectation'.

The First Sunday of Advent

Scripture-related opening prayers

Year A
God of light, dawn on us
with the new day of salvation,
and awaken your people to walk in its light.
Make your Church a gathering place of nations,
that, hearing your word, all peoples may learn
to transform the weapons of war into the tools of peace.

We ask this in the name of Jesus, the Christ,
who is one with you and the Holy Spirit,
now and for ever.

Year B
Faithful God,
from the beginning
you have formed and shaped us
like potter's clay in your hands.

Fire us with your Spirit
as vessels of your truth,
and strengthen us to the end
that we may be ready to welcome the Lord
on the day of his return in glory.

We make this prayer through Jesus Christ,
who is one with you and the Holy Spirit,
now and for ever.

Year C
God, you show your saving hand
in the midst of collapse,
and in the ending of all things
you reveal the advent of your reign.

Sharpen the senses of our spirit,
that speaking as your prophets
to interpret the signs of the times,
we may encourage others to lay aside fear
and await with us the coming of your kingdom.

We make this prayer through Jesus Christ,
who is one with you and the Holy Spirit,
now and for ever.

Opening prayer

God, our hope of glory,
inspire among your people
the strength of will for doing good,
that practising the works of justice and love
we may go to meet Christ at his coming,
and so be found worthy of a place
at his right hand in the joy of your kingdom.
We ask this in his name,
our Saviour, now and for ever.

Acclamations

Year A: Matthew 24:44
V/. Alleluia, Alleluia, Alleluia.
R/. Alleluia, Alleluia, Alleluia.
V/. You also must be ready,

for the Son of Man is coming at an unexpected hour.
R/. Alleluia, Alleluia, Alleluia.

Year B: Mark 13:31
V/. 'Heaven and earth will pass away,
but my words will not pass away.'

Year C: Luke 21:28
V/. 'Stand up and raise your heads,
because your redemption is drawing near.'

Intercession

God, for whose fullness
the whole creation is longing,
sustain your Church
in its waiting for your Christ,
so that by announcing his good news
your people may serve the coming of your kingdom.
We ask this through Jesus Christ our Lord.

Prayer over the Gifts

Bountiful God,
we prepare your feast
with gifts chosen from among your many blessings;
let these things, uplifted in thanksgiving,
bestow on us eternal redemption.
We ask this through Jesus Christ our Lord.

Eucharistic Preface

It is truly right and just,
our joy and our salvation
always and everywhere to give you thanks,
Lord, holy Father, almighty and eternal God,
through Jesus Christ our Lord.

When first he came to us
in the lowliness of our human body,
he accomplished the work you planned so long ago
and opened for us the way to salvation;
so that when he comes again in majesty and glory
your work may be completed
and we who now dare to wait in hope
may receive in its fullness
the salvation you have promised.

And so, with angels and saints,
we glorify your holy name: Holy . . .

Prayer after Communion

Lord, we pray that these gifts we have received
may teach us how to walk in this passing world
while cherishing the hope of heaven
and holding fast the blessings
that shall never pass away.
We ask this through Jesus Christ our Lord.

The Second Sunday of Advent

Scripture-related opening prayers

Year A
God of all peoples,
through the Christ, your chosen One,
you have poured out your Spirit upon all flesh.

Bring together in unity
what now in this world is divided,
so that your name may be our peace,
and our peace be your glory.

We ask this in the name of Jesus Christ,
who is one with you and the Holy Spirit,
now and for ever.

Year B
Eternal God,
in the advent of your Christ
you have laid the foundations
of a new heaven and a new earth.

Let your word of tender consolation
draw us to seek your glory,
so that we may live with hope
as citizens of your new earth,
where justice will make its home.

We ask this in the name of Jesus Christ,
who is one with you and the Holy Spirit,
now and for ever.

Year C
Eternal God,
source of all insight,
we pray to you.

Open our eyes
and let us see the vision of peace
which you place before the sight of humankind.
Set our footsteps in your path of justice
and guide us in your way of truth
so that the work you have begun
may be completed,
and all the world behold your salvation.

We ask this through Jesus Christ,
who is one with you and the Holy Spirit,
now and for ever.

Opening prayer

God of our freedom,
speed our steps as we hasten
to meet the advent of your Son;
remove the cares that block our way,
and let wisdom from on high be our teacher,
that we may walk as true companions of Christ.
We ask this in his name,
our Saviour, now and for ever.

Acclamations

Year A: Matthew 3:3
V/. Prepare the way of the Lord,
make his paths straight.

Year B: 2 Peter 3:13
V/. We wait for a new heaven and new earth,
where righteousness is at home.

Year C: Luke 3:4, 6
V/. Prepare the way of the Lord,
make his paths straight,
and all flesh shall see the salvation of God.

Intercession

All-holy God,
make your Church vigilant
and faithful in prayer,
awaiting the blessed hope
of Christ's coming in glory.
We ask this in his name,
our deliverer, now and for ever.

Prayer over the Gifts

Lord, accept our praises;
have compassion on our human frailty,
and, since we have nothing of ourselves to offer,
let your mercy make us acceptable in your sight.
We ask this through Jesus Christ our Lord.

Eucharistic Preface

The preface of the First Sunday may be used.
If an alternative preface is required more closely linked to the
appearance of John the Baptist in the readings, this might be
used:

We lift our hearts to you,
God eternal, true and faithful.
To you we offer thanks and praise
through Jesus Christ your Son.

You led your people to Christ
by the preaching of John the Baptist,
his friend and forerunner.
In the desert John prepared his way
and announced the presence of your Son,
promising his righteous judgement
and his gifts of truth and grace.

And so, with the whole assembly of heaven,
we glorify your holy name
and acclaim his coming among us,
as we sing their joyful hymn of praise: Holy . . .

Prayer after Communion

Filled with the food which nourishes the spirit
we pray to you, Lord:
grant us wisdom to live in this passing age
and inspire us with longing for the age to come.
We ask this through Jesus Christ our Lord.

The Third Sunday of Advent

Scripture-related opening prayers

Year A
All-wise God,
you are patient as your purposes unfold,
and powerful in making all things new.

Let the wonders recounted in your word
become our good news for all:
the hungry fed, the lowly raised up,
and the promises of your compassion fulfilled.

We ask this in the name of Jesus,
who is one with you and the Holy Spirit,
now and for ever.

Year B
God, our deliverer,
you bring freedom to captives
and to mourners, joy.

Let the advent of your Christ make us holy,
give gladness to the hearts of believers,
and renew the whole earth
in righteousness and praise.

We ask this in the name of Jesus,
who is one with you and the Holy Spirit,
now and for ever.

Year C
Holy God,
whose presence is unending joy,
deliver us from the cares
that oppress our minds and spirits.
Set your people free
to receive your rule and joyfully pursue
the things that lead to your peace.

We ask this through Jesus Christ,
who is one with you and the Holy Spirit,
now and for ever.

Opening prayer

Loving God,
you watch over us
as we look forward in faith
to the festival of the Lord's birth.
Bring us in peace
to that joyful feast of salvation,
that we may celebrate it
with fitting worship and heartfelt rejoicing.
We ask this in the name of Jesus Christ,
our Saviour, now and for ever.

Acclamations

Year A: Matthew 11:10
V/. See, I am sending my messenger ahead of you,
who will prepare your way before you.

Year B: Isaiah 61:1
V/. The Spirit of the Lord is upon me,
for the Lord has anointed me.

Year C: Isaiah 22:6
V/. Sing for joy, O royal Zion,
for great in your midst is the Holy One of Israel.

Intercession

Gracious God,
keep your Church close in heart
to the suffering of humanity
and the longing of peoples for justice and peace.
Let us not slacken in our pursuit of those things

that will bring all humankind
under the rule of your compassion.
We ask this through Jesus Christ our Lord.

Prayer over the Gifts

Let what we do at this table, Lord,
be a continual sacrifice of praise,
and as we proclaim the Lord's death,
accomplish your saving work among us
until his return in glory.
We ask this through Jesus Christ our Lord.

Eucharistic Preface

The preface of the First Sunday may be used.
If an alternative preface is required more closely linked to the
readings, this might be used:

It is truly right and just, our duty and our salvation,
always and everywhere to give you thanks,
Lord, holy Father, almighty and eternal God.

At your presence the lame walk
and speechless tongues are loosed in praise.
The humble are exalted, the proud are scattered.
For your way is prepared among us
and your redemption is our lasting joy
in Jesus Christ our Saviour.

And so, with the whole assembly of heaven,
we glorify your holy name
and acclaim his coming among us,
as we sing their joyful hymn of praise: Holy . . .

Prayer after Communion

Show us, Lord, your mercy,
that this gift may support us in faith,
free us from sin
and prepare us for the approaching festival.
We ask this through Jesus Christ our Lord.

The Fourth Sunday of Advent

Scripture-related opening prayers

Year A
God of wonders,
with you all things are possible.
A virgin becomes a mother
while remaining a virgin:
your eternal Word becomes a human being
while remaining one with you in glory.

Let these mysteries expand our faith,
that we may reach beyond what the eye can see
and place our hope in you alone.

We ask this through Jesus Christ,
who is one with you and the Holy Spirit,
now and for ever.

Year B
Faithful God,
you fulfilled your promise
to dwell with humankind
when the Virgin Mary gave her assent
to the message of the Angel.

Let her faith inspire your people
to welcome with joy your coming among us
and make known the mystery of your love to all.

We ask this through Jesus Christ,
who is one with you and the Holy Spirit,
now and for ever.

The Scripture-related opening prayer from Year A is also appropriate in Year B.

Year C
God of blessings,
you ask nothing of us
except to trust in your promise.

Turn us wholly to yourself,
and bestow on us the strength of will
to pledge ourselves freely to your purposes,
that your name may be glorified
to the ends of the earth.

We ask this through Jesus Christ,
who is one with you and the Holy Spirit,
now and for ever.

Opening prayer

God, abundant in blessing,
fill our hearts with your grace,
and as through the Angel's message
you announced the Incarnation of Christ your Son,
so through his passion and cross
lead us to the glory of the resurrection.
We make this prayer through Jesus Christ,
our Saviour, now and for ever.

Acclamations

Year A: Matthew 1:23
V/. The virgin shall conceive and bear a son,
and they shall name him Emmanuel.

Year B: Luke 1:38
V/. Mary said: 'I am the servant of the Lord,
let it be with me according to your word.'

Year C: Luke 1:49
V/. The Mighty One has done great things for me,
and holy is his name.

Intercession

God, our deliverer,
in the birth of Christ
your Church has its beginning.
Sustain us, as we await
his glorious coming to fulfil all things
and bring the whole creation to unity in you.
We ask this through Christ our Lord.

Prayer over the Gifts

Lord, let the Holy Spirit,
who overshadowed the blessed Virgin Mary
and made her womb fruitful,
now make our Eucharist bear abundant fruit
in the service of your kingdom.
We ask this through Christ our Lord.

Eucharistic Preface

It is truly right and just, our duty and our salvation,
always and everywhere to give you thanks,
Lord, holy Father, almighty and eternal God,
through Jesus Christ, our Lord.

Christ is the One foretold
in the words of all the prophets;
the child awaited by his virgin mother
with love that surpasses telling;

the judge whose coming John announced
and whose presence he revealed.
Now, for the feast of his nativity
Christ fills us with the joy of expectation,
that his coming may find us ready,
eager and waiting in prayer and praise to greet him.

And so, with the whole assembly of heaven,
we acclaim his coming among us,
as we sing their joyful hymn of praise: Holy . . .

or:

It is truly right and just for us to give you thanks,
to praise and bless you, here and everywhere,
creator God, the origin and end of all that is.

Your eternal Word
adorned the face of heaven with splendour
and in the glory of the Incarnation
filled the Virgin's womb and made it fruitful,
so that the radiance of new light might shine on all,
and that from Mary, Virgin and Mother,
salvation might come forth for the whole human race.

And so, throughout the heavens and the earth,
all things adore you and sing a new song;
as we, with all the angels, give you glory
in this, their ever-joyful hymn of praise: Holy . . .

Prayer after Communion

God, our hope,
grant that we, receiving the promise of redemption,
may prepare ourselves well for the coming of Christmas,
so as to celebrate worthily the mystery of your Son's birth.
We ask this through Jesus Christ our Lord.

PART TWO

PROPER TEXTS FOR CHRISTMAS, SUNDAYS AND MAJOR FESTIVALS

The Feast of Light: Themes of Christmas

Christmas is a rich and subtle festival. To study the liturgical and devotional literature of the Christmas celebration across the churches of East and West is to discover an interweaving of theological reflection and the human qualities of wonderment and awe associated with the mystery of human birth. The theme of a divine being becoming human as a helpless infant still exercises a fascination. The development of this feast is almost as fascinating as its literature.

The early Latin liturgical texts, the collects and prefaces, coming as they do from some of the great pastors and preachers of the fifth and sixth centuries of the Christian Era, focus on the dogmatic and theological aspects of the celebration. From later periods, however, we have the many carols, poems and hymns that speak of the Christmas events from a human and emotional perspective. The Christmas Crib, whose invention is credited to Francis of Assisi, also captures that emerging human interest which typified the iconography of the later medieval period. Such human interest does not necessarily detract from the dogmatic assertions of Christmas. It can serve to reinforce the wondrous nature of the Incarnation. In true Franciscan spirit, John Donne expressed the sense of compassion for the lowliness of God amongst us, when with complete orthodoxy he wrote:

Seest thou, my soul, with thy faith's eyes, how he
Which fills all place, yet none holds him, doth lie?
Was not his pity towards thee wondrous high
That would have need to be pitied by thee?

Christmas has a quality of wonder and 'make-believe' about it which reflects the character of the 'infancy narratives' in the Gospels of Matthew and Luke. Modern scriptural scholarship has carefully exposed the complex nature of these stories, their sources and theological focus. It is clear that in different ways the Synoptic Gospels made use of the rich messianic traditions of the Jewish scriptures to express in narrative form the dogmatic truth of Jesus as the Christ of God, Son of David, Son of Adam and child of the Virgin Mary by the overshadowing of the Most High. It is perhaps hard for modern readers to make the same theological sense of the details as the original tellers of the stories were making. It is beyond doubt, however, that the images presented in the opening chapters of Matthew and Luke have established themselves firmly as a memorable and captivating narrative.

In a quite different way, the beautiful and profound hymn that forms the prologue to the Gospel according to Saint John speaks of Jesus Christ as the enfleshment of the pre-existent Word and celebrates that human flesh as the Light enlightening all people, the Light that darkness could not overcome. The Fourth Gospel tells a quite different story from the infancy narratives of Matthew and Luke. Where the Synoptics make a vivid appeal to the eye, the Fourth Gospel appeals sonorously to the ear. Matthew and Luke paint very human scenes, the Fourth Gospel speaks profoundly of the essence of God. Where Matthew traces Jesus' ancestry to Abraham as Son of David and Luke traces his genealogy to Adam as Son of Man, John unfolds his eternal identity 'In the beginning . . .' as the Son of God.

This prologue to the Fourth Gospel is central to the celebration of Christmas, because, though it does not recall Christ's human birth directly, it acts as a sort of commentary upon it and speaks more deeply about the ultimate meaning of Christmas, which is the coming and the glory of the Word made Flesh. *We saw his glory, the glory as of the Only Begotten of the Father, full of grace and truth* (John 1:14). The Incarnation was the gift planned *before the foundation of the world* (Ephesians 1:4) so that the One who was *The image of the invisible God, the firstborn of all creation* (Colossians 1:15) might become in his human nature *The head of the body, the Church; the beginning, the firstborn from the dead* (Colossians 1:18).

Throughout the Christmas Season, Saint John's theme of the light is prominent in prayers and other texts. Again and again we are invited to reflect, not on the outward details of the Christmas story, but on its deeper meaning as a revelation of divine uncreated light. As Cardinal Newman so strikingly put it in his great hymn 'Praise to the Holiest in the Height', this is that 'higher gift than grace'. At Christmas we remember the advent, not of 'grace', God in abstract, as it were, but of God's very self.

Another deeper theme of Christmas is that of the 'divine exchange' – a reflection on the ancient teaching of the Catholic Church that our Lord Jesus Christ is fully God and fully Man, and that this in some way forms the beginning of an exchange between the human and the divine, whereby (in the words of a Christmas preface) the Word made Flesh, whom we can see, will lead us to contemplate what is unseen, the mystery of the Trinity itself; or (in the words of a Christmas prayer): 'as Christ became a sharer in our human nature, so humanity may share in the divine nature'.

Yet a third set of themes in the prayers of the Christmas Season are the Easter themes of new life and rebirth and freedom from the 'ancient yoke of our sinfulness'. It is as if the Christmas story is a retelling of the Easter story in another guise. A link with the Easter celebration was already being made by some of the great 'Fathers' of the Church as early as the fifth century AD. Christmas is sometimes spoken of as the 'Winter Passover', a rehearsal of Easter in what is (at least in the northern hemisphere) the darkest and coldest time of the year.

The Christmas round of services nowadays usually includes a Midnight Mass or Communion. It is surprising how quickly this has taken root in the Church of England, and how it has spread far beyond the 'high church' parishes that first started it. In his history of Westminster Abbey, Jocelyn Perkins tells how, in 1941, with the war raging and Government employees at their desks late into the night on Christmas Eve behind the Whitehall blackout, the Abbey authorities arranged a Communion service at midnight so that some of them, at least, should not miss Christmas Communion. The blackout meant that the only lights in the Abbey were the candles on the altar, and the carols were sung from memory. It must have been a memorable event.

In fact, 'Midnight' is a fairly recent hour for the first Christmas Eucharist. The ancestor of our 'Midnight Mass' is the Mass entitled Mass 'At Cockcrow' in the Sarum Missal. 'Cockcrow' probably indicated that the Mass was sung between the two night services of Matins and Lauds. The Sarum Use was derived from the Roman liturgy, and in medieval Rome a second Mass was sung at daybreak and the Mass of Christmas Day later in the morning.

Historically, the Mass of Christmas Day is the most important of the Christmas Masses and the most ancient. By its choice of biblical readings and prayers this liturgy proclaims the Church's dogma of the person and nature of Christ, the eternal Word. The earliest sources for the Roman Church indicate that this Mass took place at the Basilica of Saint Peter, the Tomb of the Apostle on the Vatican Hill. Later missals place it in the Basilica of Santa Maria Maggiore, the first church in the city dedicated to the Mother of God.

The Night Mass also took place at Santa Maria Maggiore, in a chapel known as 'The Manger' where the reputed relics of Jesus' birth crib were venerated. The Dawn Mass took place at a smaller church dedicated to Saint Anastasia, probably a third-century martyr whose commemoration, on 25 December, was also mentioned in the prayers of the Mass.

Nowadays, however, it is the Midnight Mass that is likely to be the principal Eucharist of Christmas.

The Common Worship *Lectionary gives three sets of readings*

for the Eucharist or Main Service on Christmas Day. Any set
may be used at any time, but the third set should always be used.
The Scripture-related prayers given here follow the pattern set
out in the Lectionary.

Christmas Day

Prayers appropriate for a Midnight Service

Scripture-related opening prayer

God of wonders,
on this most holy night
your grace has appeared to humankind,
for by a lowly birth, your eternal Word
has come to live as one of us.

Let the life of Christ
be the life of Christians:
let Christ's death be their new birth
and Christ's Gospel, their inspiration.
So shall you receive glory,
and the whole earth be held in your peace.

We make this prayer through Jesus Christ,
who is one with you and the Holy Spirit,
now and for ever.

Opening prayer

Eternal God,
who at the world's midnight
sent Wisdom from heaven
to pitch a tent on earth,
let the glory which heralded his coming
be kindled again among your people
and the peace of which the angels sang
be shown forth in the lives of those who believe.

We ask this through Jesus Christ,
who is one with you and the Holy Spirit,
now and for ever.

Acclamation

Luke 2:34
V/. Alleluia, Alleluia, Alleluia.
R/. Alleluia, Alleluia, Alleluia.
Glory to God in the highest,
and peace on earth.
R/. Alleluia, Alleluia, Alleluia.

Intercession

Gracious God,
you make us your children in Christ.
May the birth of Jesus
strengthen our hope in your promise
of a humanity renewed in his likeness,
for he is Lord for ever and ever.

Prayer over the Gifts

Lord, let praise and thanksgiving
be the pure offering of this day's feast,
and as your eternal Word takes up our human nature,
so by a holy exchange
may we be taken up into the divine life of Christ,
who is alive, now and for ever.

Eucharistic Preface

It is truly right and just, our duty and our salvation,
always and everywhere to give you thanks,
Lord, holy Father, almighty and eternal God,
through Jesus Christ our Lord.

In the mystery of the Word made Flesh,
your everlasting light has shone
with new and radiant splendour in our midst,
so that as we see our God made visible,
we may be caught up in love
of the things that are invisible.

And so, with angels and archangels,
and with all the powers of heaven,
we glorify your holy name
in this, their ageless hymn of praise: Holy . . .

or:

It is truly right and just, our duty and our salvation,
always and everywhere to give you thanks,
Lord, holy Father, almighty and eternal God,
through Jesus Christ our Lord.

Today is the birthday of the Saviour
and the beginning of our salvation,
since by the coming of Christ
the world is reborn,
resurrection is given to the dead
and immortal life restored to mortals.

And so, with angels and archangels,
and with all the powers of heaven,
we glorify your holy name
in this, their ageless hymn of praise: Holy . . .

Prayer after Communion

God, whose table we have shared,
grant that as we rejoice to celebrate
the birth of our Redeemer,
so through your gift of holiness
we may be made capable of receiving his glory.
We ask this through Christ our Lord.

Prayers appropriate early on Christmas Morning

Scripture-related opening prayer

God of tender compassion,
whose love has dawned upon us
in the birth of Jesus,
remember this work of your grace
and establish your Church
as a holy people
saved by your mercy
and heir to eternal life.

We ask this through Jesus Christ,
who is one with you and the Holy Spirit,
now and for ever.

Opening prayer

Almighty God,
neither heaven nor earth can hold you,
yet in a little space, a woman's womb,
your incarnate Word made an earthly dwelling.
Consecrate us, by the new birth of baptism,
to be a temple of your glory
and make our lives transparent
to your wisdom, compassion and grace.
We ask this through our Saviour Jesus Christ,
who is one with you and the Holy Spirit,
now and for ever.

Acclamation

V/. Alleluia, Alleluia, Alleluia.
R/. Alleluia, Alleluia, Alleluia.
V/. Today a holy day has dawned upon us,
come you nations to the light of the Lord.
R/. Alleluia, Alleluia, Alleluia.

Intercession

Let the praises of your people
rise before your glory, Lord,
so that the peace announced by the angels
may truly be established
and all peoples enjoy your favour.
We ask this through Christ, our Lord.

Prayer over the Gifts

God, give us words
to make our thanksgiving
worthy of this holy day,
and just as this human birth has revealed
the One who is God among us,
so let these earthly gifts
bestow on us the gifts of heaven.
We ask this through Christ our Lord.

Eucharistic Preface

It is truly right and just, our duty and our salvation,
always and everywhere to give you thanks,
Lord, holy Father, almighty and eternal God,
through Jesus Christ our Lord.

In Christ there has shone forth for us
the wonderful exchange that brings salvation;
for when your Word takes on our human frailty,
our mortal nature assumes immortal honour,
and we, through this wonderful union,
are clothed in eternal life.

And so, with angels and archangels,
and with all the powers of heaven,
we glorify your holy name
in this, their ageless hymn of praise: Holy . . .

Prayer after Communion

Gracious God,
give us joy in the nativity of your Son,
that we may grasp this mystery with wholehearted faith,
and hold to it with an ever growing love.
We ask this through Christ our Lord.

Prayers appropriate to Christmas Day

Scripture-related opening prayer

Great and gracious God,
from the beginning
you have spoken to us,
and now, your eternal Word
has made a dwelling among us,
changing the shadows of our earthly being
into the bright morning of heaven's glory.

Let us receive him again in faith and hope,
so that we and all who welcome him
may know the wonder of being called your children.

We ask this in his name,
who is one with you and the Holy Spirit,
now and for ever.

Opening prayer

Almighty God,
you gave a wonderful dignity
to the human race that you created:
you bestowed an even more wonderful destiny
on that same humanity restored in Christ.
Grant that we may be partakers of his divine nature
just as he humbled himself to share in our humanity.
We ask this through Jesus Christ,

who is one with you and the Holy Spirit
now and for ever.

Acclamation

John 1:14
V/. Alleluia, Alleluia, Alleluia.
R/. Alleluia, Alleluia, Alleluia.
V/. The Word was made flesh,
and dwelt among us.
R/. Alleluia, Alleluia, Alleluia.

Intercession

God our glory,
let the world be filled with your splendour
and all nations come to know your salvation.
We ask this through Christ our Lord.

Prayer over the Gifts

Lord, let this day's Eucharist
unite us to Christ,
in whose self-offering
you have brought us reconciliation
with the fullness of worship and praise.
We ask this through Christ our Lord.

Eucharistic Preface

The first of the Christmas prefaces on pp. 25–6 may be used.

or:

It is truly right and just, our duty and our salvation,
always and everywhere to give you thanks,
Lord, holy Father, almighty and eternal God,
through Jesus Christ our Lord.

In the mystery of Christmas
the One who as God is invisible
has now appeared as one like us,
and the One begotten before the ages
begins to exist in time.
He comes to raise what was fallen,
to restore creation to wholeness
and lead a lost humanity
back to the kingdom of heaven.

And so, with angels and archangels,
and with all the powers of heaven,
we glorify your holy name
in this, their ageless hymn of praise: Holy . . .

Prayer after Communion

Grant, O merciful God,
that as the Saviour of the world born this day
is the author of our heavenly birth,
so likewise he may bestow on us
the gift of immortality.
For he is alive, now and for ever.

*For the feasts of Saint Stephen, Deacon and Martyr, Saint John
the Evangelist and the Holy Innocents, please see pp. 142–9.*

*For 1 January: The Octave Day of Christmas and Festival of the
Circumcision of Jesus, see the prayers on pp. 149–51.*

The First Sunday of Christmas

Scripture-related opening prayers

Year A
Eternal God,
for whom all things exist,
you have given your Son Jesus Christ

to be one with us in flesh and blood
and through his dying and rising
to become the author of our eternal life.

Grant that we may find him close to us
as our strength in suffering,
our sure intercessor
and our trustworthy guide
on the road to eternal life.

We ask this in his name,
for he is one with you and the Holy Spirit,
now and for ever.

Year B
God, our salvation,
you have sent the Spirit of your Son into our heart.

By that same Spirit, inspire in us
the trust and joy of your children,
so that our minds may ponder your word,
and our lives give you glory and praise.

We ask this in the name of Jesus,
who is one with you and the Holy Spirit,
now and for ever.

Year C
God of all grace,
you have chosen us in Christ to be your people.

Teach us the ways of your wisdom,
that the word of Christ may dwell in us,
the peace of Christ rule our hearts
and the love of Christ bind us together
in a harmony of gratitude and praise.

We ask this in the name of Christ,
who is one with you and the Holy Spirit,
now and for ever.

Opening prayer

All-powerful God,
grant in your mercy
that we, who are held in our ancient slavery
to the powers of death,
may be set free by the new birth
of your Only-Begotten Son.
We ask this in his name,
who is alive, now and for ever.

Acclamation

John 1:14
V/. Alleluia, Alleluia, Alleluia.
R/. Alleluia, Alleluia, Alleluia.
V/. The Word was made flesh,
and dwelt among us.
R/. Alleluia, Alleluia, Alleluia.

Intercession

Gracious God,
bestir your people
to sing the angels' song of glory
and actively to seek
the peace which they proclaimed,
so that you may be truly glorified.
We ask this through Christ our Lord.

Prayer over the Gifts

Eternal God,
in the Word made flesh
you joined together heaven and earth.
Make us holy by sharing in this table
and make us joyful in giving you praise.
We ask this through Jesus Christ our Lord.

Eucharistic Preface

We lift our hearts to you,
God eternal, good and faithful;
to you we offer thanks and praise
in the name of Jesus Christ.

We celebrate the wonder of the Incarnation,
by which our human state
is freed from its ancient earthly destiny
and raised up in Christ to a new and heavenly birth.

And so, with boundless joy,
your Church is united to the praises of heaven
as we praise your holy name and say: Holy . . .

Prayer after Communion

God of glory,
you have revealed your Christ
as the light of the world.
By this communion,
renew us in the love of Christ
and in witness to his Gospel.
We ask this through Christ our Lord.

The Second Sunday of Christmas

Scripture-related opening prayer

Years ABC
God of blessings,
in Christ you have become a father to us,
and have destined us for the redemption
that is ours through his blood.

Let us bear faithfully
the seal of your Holy Spirit,
and live blameless lives

for the praise of your glory
and the consoling of the world.

We ask this in the name of Jesus,
who is one with you and the Holy Spirit,
now and for ever.

Opening prayer

God of unfailing light,
splendour of all who believe,
let the whole world see your glory
and all peoples know your saving help.
We ask this through Jesus Christ, the Lord.

Acclamation

John 1:18
V/. It is God the only Son, who is close to the Father's heart,
who has made him known.

Intercession

God, our salvation,
prosper the mission of your Church,
that the world may acknowledge
its freedom and redemption
in the name of Jesus,
who is alive, now and for ever.

Prayer over the Gifts

Lord, sanctify the table we prepare
as we celebrate the nativity of your Only-Begotten Son,
for by this holy birth
you display your truth among us
and show us the way of salvation.
We ask this in the name of Jesus Christ.

Eucharistic Preface

It is truly right and just to praise you,
the almighty and eternal God,
and to offer you the sacrifice of thanksgiving.

This is the pure offering
promised in the sacrifice of righteous Abel
and foreshadowed in the Passover Lamb,
the sacrifice foretold in Abraham's obedience,
and in the gift of Melchizedek the priest:
here is all worship,
perfected and fulfilled in Christ,
who by his own self-offering
has brought us reconciliation
and given you perfect praise.

Through Christ, the angels acclaim you
and the powers of heaven stand in awe;
unite us with them, as we proclaim
their ageless hymn of praise: Holy . . .

Prayer after Communion

God of justice,
grant that this holy mystery may work within us,
to root out wickedness
and fulfil our desire for what is good.
We ask this through Christ, our Lord.

The Epiphany of Christ

The feast of Epiphany completes the Christmas story. In the tradition of the Prayer Book the Epiphany seems primarily to commemorate the visit of the Magi to the infant Jesus and their gifts
of gold, incense and myrrh. In all the traditions deriving from the
Roman Church's practice, this theme provides the focus of the
Eucharistic readings for the day. However, the greater part of the

Christian world, both the 'Eastern' churches and those of France and Spain in the very early medieval period, celebrated the Baptism of Christ as the first of the Epiphany stories, followed by the sign of his divinity given by Jesus at Cana in Galilee.

All this is consistent with the meaning of the word itself, which is Greek for 'appearance', meaning both a revelation and also a formal visitation. At the Baptism of Jesus, the Father and the Holy Spirit were revealed, and thus in Christian thinking Epiphany is a manifestation of the Trinity, and also of the mission of the Son of God.

Two sets of prayers are given here, for a Vigil Eucharist and for the Eucharist or main service of the day.

The Vigil of Epiphany

The Common Worship Lectionary does not offer any readings for an Epiphany Vigil. Some possible choices are suggested with the prayers given here, which might be used at an evening service on 5 January. See also the form for an Epiphany Vigil, pp. 64–7.

Opening prayer

God revealed in Christ,
let the splendour of your glory
flood our hearts and minds,
that we may learn to worship
in spirit and in truth.

We make this prayer through Jesus Christ,
who is one with you and the Holy Spirit,
now and for ever.

Old Testament Reading: Isaiah 55:1–5

Psalm 87

New Testament Reading: Romans 3:27–31

Acclamation

John 4:24
V/. God is spirit, and those who worship him
must worship him in spirit and in truth.

Gospel Reading: John 4:19–26

Intercession

Show to your people, Lord,
the light of your truth,
and as you have called your Church
to be a light for the world,
so fill your people with the wisdom
to bear that light for your glory.
We ask this through Jesus Christ our Lord.

Prayer over the Gifts

God of all peoples,
at your table no one is a stranger.
open our mouths to sing your praise
and our hearts to welcome our neighbour.
We ask this through Jesus Christ our Lord.

Eucharistic Preface

It is truly right and just, our duty and our salvation,
always and everywhere to give you thanks,
Lord, holy Father, almighty and eternal God,
through Jesus Christ our Lord.

Most of all, in this holy mystery do we praise you,
because the true light of our Saviour has shone forth,
restoring to us all the life we had lost.

This is the light that shines in splendour
to guide us on our pilgrim way
and lead us to the contemplation
of his glory and boundless majesty.

And so, with angels and saints,
we sing the unending hymn of your glory: Holy . . .

Prayer after Communion

Purify our hearts, O God,
so that in the strength of this holy food
we may perceive with the eye of faith
what you have revealed to us in Christ.
We ask this through Christ our Lord.

The Day of Epiphany

Scripture-related opening prayer

Years ABC
God of earth and heaven,
you have revealed the mystery of Christ
to every people and nation.

Inspire your Church
to make known the riches of your saving purpose,
so that from the rising of the sun to its setting,
all peoples may lift up a pure offering
to the glory of your name.

We ask this through Jesus Christ,
who is one with you and the Holy Spirit,
now and for ever.

Opening prayer

God of all peoples,
you consecrated this day

by calling the first of the gentile nations
to follow Christ as the bright star of morning
and adore him as the Word made Flesh.
Let the light of Christian faith
so illuminate the life of your people
that all may see our good works
and give you the glory.
We make this prayer through Jesus Christ,
who is one with you and the Holy Spirit,
now and for ever.

Acclamation

Matthew 2:2b
V/. We observed his star at its rising
and have come to pay him homage.

Intercession

Bless your Church, Lord,
and inspire its witness
to the presence and work of Christ.
Strengthen its weakness
and guide it to follow
the light of faith which you have kindled.
We ask this through Christ our Lord.

*If gold, incense and myrrh are presented as part of the ritual of
preparing the eucharistic table, the following prayer is not used.
In its place the Prayer over the Gifts given on p. 136 is said.*

Prayer over the Gifts

In your kindness, Lord,
look upon the gifts of your Church.
We bring no gold now,
no frankincense or myrrh,
but we celebrate the One

whose risen life these gifts proclaim:
Christ Jesus your Son,
who is alive, now and for ever.

Eucharistic Preface

It is truly right and just, our duty and our salvation,
always and everywhere to give you thanks,
Lord, holy Father, almighty and eternal God,
through Jesus Christ our Lord.

From the moment of his wondrous birth,
your eternal Word
revealed his power by signs and marvels.
By a star he guided the Wise Men,
at Cana he changed the water into wine,
and at his baptism made Jordan's water holy.
By these great mysteries of salvation
we have come to know your purpose
to live among us in the person of your beloved Son;
to be for us the way to eternal joy,
the truth in whose light we may clearly see,
the fountain of life that springs up eternally in Christ.

And so, in the song of angels,
we glorify your holy name: Holy . . .

or:

It is truly right and just, our duty and our salvation,
always and everywhere to give you thanks,
Lord, holy Father, almighty and eternal God,
through Jesus Christ our Lord.

Because on this day you revealed
the mystery of our salvation in Christ,
the light of nations;
and now that he has appeared,
incarnate in our mortal flesh,

you have created us anew in the glory
of his immortal life.

And so, with angels and archangels
and with all the powers of heaven,
we glorify your holy name
in this, their ageless hymn of praise: Holy . . .

Prayer after Communion

Go before us, Lord, we pray,
always and everywhere with your celestial light,
that we may discern with a clear mind
and receive with pure affection
the mystery you have called us here to share.
We ask this through Christ our Lord.

The Baptism of Christ

The Eastern churches celebrate the Baptism of Christ at Epiphany,
as the manifestation of the Son of God. In the early Middle
Ages, those Latin-speaking churches independent liturgically of
the Roman Church seem to have done the same. In the eighth
century, the churches influenced by the Roman Liturgy began to
commemorate the Baptism of the Lord during the days following
Epiphany. The feast became part of the Sunday cycle of the
Roman Catholic Church in 1960, and *The Alternative Service
Book* fixed it on the Sunday after Epiphany in 1980.

Scripture-related opening prayers

Year A
God, our Father,
whose beloved Son was eager to receive
the baptism of repentance
so that your justice might be fulfilled,
grant that, as he chose to be one with sinners,

so we who became one with him in baptism
may follow him in the service of your justice
and in the proclamation of your gospel.

We ask this through Jesus Christ,
who is one with you and the Holy Spirit,
now and for ever.

Year B
At the beginning of creation, O God,
your Spirit swept over the waters,
and at the Baptism of Jesus, your Son,
that same Spirit came down
to anoint him as the Christ.

Grant that all your baptized people
may recognize their Christian dignity
and so live as to be found worthy of it.

We ask this through Jesus Christ,
who is one with you and the Holy Spirit,
for ever and ever.

Year C
God of glory,
in the Baptism of your beloved Son
you revealed the anointing of the Spirit
and foretold the baptism that is to come.

Let us not fear the closeness of your judgement
but rather, by good and faithful discipleship,
let us prepare on earth the foundations
of your heavenly kingdom,
so that when, on that last day,
your voice will shake the universe,
we may stand with joy to welcome
the One who is to come and bless us with peace;
Jesus Christ, whose reign is for ever and ever.

Opening prayer

Gracious God,
through the Holy Spirit
you have revealed to us
the one who is your servant and your Son.
We pray you,
that as we have been baptized into his death,
so we may be kept faithful
in our witness to his resurrection,
for he is alive, and glorious for ever and ever.

Acclamation

Years ABC
V/. Alleluia, Alleluia, Alleluia.
R/. Alleluia, Alleluia, Alleluia.
V/. The heavens were opened and the voice of the Father was
heard:
'This is my Son, the Beloved; the One on whom my favour rests.'
R/. Alleluia, Alleluia, Alleluia.

Intercession

Holy God,
let your abundant blessing
descend from heaven upon your Church,
to confirm and create anew
those who in the sacrament of Baptism
have been washed in water
and born again in the life-giving Spirit.
We ask this through Jesus Christ our Lord.

Prayer over the Gifts

Gracious God,
we come with bread and wine,
with thanksgiving and praise,

to the table you prepare
for your baptized people.
Through your Holy Spirit,
let us enter here into the fellowship of Christ
and into the movement of his self-offering,
for he is alive, now and for ever.

Eucharistic Preface

It is truly right and just, our duty and our salvation,
always and everywhere to give you thanks,
Lord, holy Father, almighty and eternal God.

In the voice from heaven over the Jordan river
you revealed yourself as the Saviour of all
and the Father of the eternal Light.
You rent the heavens, blessed the air
and purified the springs of water;
then by the Holy Spirit in form of a dove descending
you announced the advent of your Only-Begotten Son.
Today the waters received your blessing,
to wash away our ancient curse,
to grant believers the forgiveness of sins
and make them your very own children
by a heavenly birth into eternal life.

And so, with all creation on this joyful feast,
we acclaim you, the source of life and goodness,
in this holy and exultant song: Holy . . .

Prayer after Communion

Years ABC
God, our provider,
let us walk in the strength of this food
as children of your light,
so that both in title and in truth
we may truly be your beloved sons and daughters.
We ask this through Christ our Lord.

PART THREE

TEXTS FOR VIGIL SERVICES FOR SUNDAYS AND MAJOR FESTIVALS

Christians keep Sunday sacred because it is the 'Lord's Day' – the day of the resurrection of Christ. It is traditional in Anglican worship and in many other historic traditions to begin the celebration of Sunday at Evening Prayer on Saturday. This tradition might be expressed by the solemn celebration of Saturday Evening Prayer with a Service of Light and Incense, or the celebration of a Saturday evening Vigil Service for Sunday. In this section, prayers and other material are proposed which might form part of such a service.

Every Sunday is 'The Lord's Day', the day when Jesus rose from the dead 'as Lord and Christ' (Acts 2:36). The Sundays of Advent and Christmas are equally celebrations of the Risen Christ, but having their particular seasonal 'colour'. Since all Christian celebration is based in the crucified, risen and glorified Christ, Christian tradition has been able to perceive a strong paschal reference in Advent and Christmas.

The Christmas Season transcends its 'historical' setting. It is both the remembrance of the birth of Christ, and a contemporary, paschal celebration of new birth for those who believe in him and who are united to his dying and rising through faith and the sacrament of baptism. Its temporal transcendence extends retrospectively into Advent, which takes on the form of a time looking forward from the present to the 'age to come', to the return of the Risen One in glory. For Christian celebration, therefore, whatever the 'historic' mode of the story, the strong 'present tense' of both Advent and Christmas is always that of Easter.

It is traditional to begin the first evening prayer or vigil of Sundays and festivals with a Service of Light. The service might also include a Rite of Incense as a celebration of the resurrection and a prayer for forgiveness and purification. In the Byzantine Liturgy, Vespers is celebrated with the burning of incense, during which parts of Psalm 141 are sung. To these verses are attached hymns celebrating the risen life of Christ.

In this section, chants for the services of Light and Incense are included, as in Volumes I and II. In addition, a lectionary for the vigils of Christmas, Epiphany and the Baptism of Christ is suggested. More general indications are given for the celebration of a Sunday Vigil Service.

Groups intending to celebrate a vigil will need to plan its 'choreography' and decide how they are to use light, incense (if desired) and other symbols, how the assembly space is to be laid out, how the readings are to be presented, if audio or visual aids are to be used, and so on. Since the aim of a vigil is to listen to and reflect upon the Word of God, allowing it to sink into the heart, the space where it is celebrated, the pacing and the manner of its celebration need to be carefully considered beforehand.

The Service of Light

Common Worship – Daily Prayer *(Church House Publishing 2002) makes provision also for this on pp. 84ff.*

The leader opens the service with the words:

In the name of our Lord Jesus Christ,
light and peace be with you all.

All reply:

And also with you.

Lights are kindled as required. The Easter Candle may be used, or the candles lit on the Advent wreath.

A hymn of praise to Christ, or a seasonal hymn, might be sung here. The traditional evening hymn for Advent is 'Creator of the stars of night' (New English Hymnal 1). An alternative might be:

An Advent Hymn
(This may be sung to the plainsong tune of 'Creator of the stars of night')

All glorious from the eastern skies
The aspect of the noble king:
The Christ, creation's light and Lord,
Alpha and Omega, shall come.

In this, the evening of the day,
The evening of the turning year,
We turn our songs to his return
Whose light enlightens all that live.

The Son of Man in glory comes
To judge the living and the dead;
The Bridegroom has prepared the Bride
With joy to take her for his own.

Come, Sun of Justice, Light of life,
Come, Lord of ages and of time,
Open the doors to Heaven's hall
And usher in the wedding feast.

Other choices for Advent:

The advent of our God (New English Hymnal 14)
Wake, O wake! (New English Hymnal 16)
The King shall come when morning dawns (Laudate 106)

For Christmas:

*Come, thou Redeemer of the earth (*New English Hymnal *19)*
*Of the Father's heart begotten (*New English Hymnal *33)*

For Epiphany and the Baptism of Christ:

*The race that long in darkness pined (*New English Hymnal *57)*

Prayer to conclude the Service of Light

Advent
Christ, our true light,
you will come at an hour we do not expect.
Keep us vigilant in the night
with lamps prepared and shining
to welcome you, the Bridegroom,
when you return for the eternal wedding feast,
where you will be the fulfilment of all our desire,
for ever and ever.

Christmas Eve
God, lover of humankind,
in the night of this present age
we await the coming of your Only-Begotten Son.
Illuminate our faith,
that we may acknowledge the newborn Christ
and, with the angels, proclaim his praise.
We ask this through Jesus Christ our Lord.

Christmas Season
Word made Flesh,
you are the light
that gives radiance to all creation
and enlightens the minds and hearts of all.
Let us acknowledge you as Son of God
that we may know ourselves
as your brothers and sisters,
co-heirs with you of eternal light,

for you are one with the Father and the Holy Spirit,
now and for ever.

Epiphany and the Baptism of Christ
God, our light,
whose glory has risen upon us,
let nations come to you,
seeking the brightness of your light,
that all may acknowledge you as the one true God,
through the Christ whom you have sent.
For he is one with you,
in the unity of the Holy Spirit,
now and for ever.

The Service of Incense

*The refrain is always from Psalm 141:2, set to different melodies.
One set of verses is suggested here for each of the Sundays of
Advent and Christmas, for Christmas itself, the Circumcision,
Epiphany and the Baptism of Christ.*

First Sunday of Advent

Refrain:

Let my prayer— rise like in - - cense;
my up - lift - ed hands as the eve - ning sac - ri - fice.

Tone:

Verses:

O risen Lord, let this our evening prayer
Arise like fragrant incense in your sight;
You are the living One who died and rose,
Revealing resurrection to the world.

As you ascended, so you will return
In glory with the bright angelic host;
From heaven like the blazing, rising sun
In clouds of glory you will come again.

Behold the Bridegroom! Let us keep awake
With lamps alight that will not fade or fail;
At midnight he may come, or at the dawn,
His coming certain, but the hour unknown.

Let all adore the Lord and sing his praise,
And glorify his resurrection from the dead;
Christ is our Lord and God who trampled down
Our ancient and deceitful enemy.

To Christ who in the flesh bore death for us,
Who rose in glory, glorious to return,
We pray: 'Confirm your Church in truth and praise,
Give peace to all, O friend of humankind!'

Second Sunday of Advent

Refrain:

Let my prayer— rise like in - cense;
my up - lift - ed hands as the eve - ning sac - ri - fice.

Tone:

Verses:

Come let us worship Christ the Son of God,
The First-Begotten, now of Mary born;
Who by his own free will accepted death.
Praise be to you, the One who is to come!

In truth we hold that you will come again,
With justice for the living and the dead;
All that lies hidden then will be revealed.
Praise be to you, the One who is to come!

John the Baptizer heralded your reign,
Preaching repentance in the cleansing waters;
But we have been baptized into your death,
Praise be to you, the One who is to come!

When all in heaven and on earth profess
That you are God and Saviour of them all,
The just will shine like stars in heaven and say:
Praise be to you, the One who is to come!

With all creation's powers let us praise
The rising of the Lord who saves our souls;
For he will come again to judge the world:
Praise be to you, the One who is to come!

Third Sunday of Advent

Refrain:

Let my prayer rise like in - - cense;
my up-lift-ed hands as the eve-ning sac-ri-fice.

Tone:

Verses:

You broke the grip of death, O Christ our Saviour,
When on the cross you foiled our ancient foe;
By faith you save us and to faith you call us,
Praise be to you, the One who is to come!

Rejoice! Rejoice with gladness in the Lord
And praise his resurrection from the dead;
With songs of joy let all creation sound:
Praise be to you, the One who is to come!

The universe will tremble at your coming,
Before your judgement seat a fire devours;
The books are opened, secrets are disclosed.
Praise be to you, the One who is to come!

When first you came in lowliness to earth,
Your Godhead, hidden, still as God remained;
For you are the eternal, uncreated Word;
Praise be to you, the One who is to come!

Amid your Church, O Christ our God, we bless you
And offer up our evening hymns of praise;
O Christ, the friend of humankind, the Risen One,
Praise be to you, the One who is to come!

Fourth Sunday of Advent

Refrain:

Let my prayer rise like in - - cense; my up-lift-ed hands as the eve-ning sac-ri-fice.

Tone:

Verses:

Come, let us sing our Saviour's resurrection
And with the angels praise and thank the Lord;
Who brought us out of death to incorruption
And shed his glorious light on humankind.

To Bethlehem we lift our hearts and minds,
Awaiting the Nativity of Christ;
The Virgin comes to bear the promised child,
The Lord of all he is and Christ our God.

Heaven give heed! Earth, listen and behold!
The Word eternal comes to human birth;
And He Who Is becomes what he was not,
To fill creation with the life of God.

Your coming from the Father is eternal,
Your Incarnation is beyond all power to tell;
Your advent to the dead strikes death with terror,
For now you have destroyed its pain and fear.

Glory to you, O Christ, Incarnate Word!
One person, truly God and truly Man!
Two natures in one person, you we hold
One Lord, one Christ, one Saviour of us all.

Christmas

Refrain:

Let my prayer— rise like in - cense; my up-lift-ed hands as the eve-ning sac-ri-fice.

Tone:

Verses:

Let us rejoice to tell the Mystery:
The gate of Paradise is opened wide,
The cherubim withdraw the flaming sword,
The Tree of Life offers to us its fruit.

The Image of the Father, Christ our God
Assumes a servant's form yet changes not;
And from the Virgin Mother issues forth
To fill the world with God's eternal light.

True God he is, true God he will remain,
Yet takes upon himself what he was not;
And out of love for fallen humankind
Mortal becomes, to save mortality.

Our Saviour has appeared in human flesh
To fill the universe with holy light;
The shepherds see his glory and adore,
Wise men are guided by a star to Christ.

Your rule, O Christ our God, will last for ever,
Your coming has made light to shine on all;
You are the image of the Father's glory
Who from the Virgin's womb have sprung today.

The Sunday after Christmas

Refrain:

Let my prayer rise like in - - cense; my up - lift - ed hands as the eve - ning sac - ri - fice.

Tone:

Verses:
You broke the power of death, Lord Jesus Christ,
When on the cross you offered up your life;
And by your glorious rising from the dead
You led us forth from darkness into light.

Led to the slaughter like a spotless lamb
You are our Passover of life and peace;
You went into the darkest realm of death
To set its captives free and lead them forth.

Praise to the Shepherd who became the Lamb!
Praise to the grain that is our living bread!
Praise to the vine that is our saving cup!
Who by his birth brings hope to all the world.

Our Saviour has appeared in human flesh
To fill the universe with holy light;
The shepherds see his glory and adore,
Wise men are guided by a star to Christ.

O Light undying, hear our evening praise,
For you have filled the universe with light;
Your light divine transforms our human flesh
And shines for ever, mirrored in your saints.

The Feast of the Circumcision

Refrain:

Let my prayer rise like in - - cense; my up - lift - ed hands as the eve - ning sac - ri - fice.

Tone:

Verses:

The Image of the Father, Christ our God
Assumes a servant's form yet changes not;
And from the Virgin Mother issues forth
To fill the world with God's eternal light.

He gave the Law, now he that Law obeys,
Accepting circumcision in the flesh;
To save us all he gives this saving sign:
He lives as one of us in all but sin.

True God he is, true God he will remain,
Yet takes upon himself what he was not;
And out of love for fallen humankind
Mortal becomes, to save mortality.

Blessed is Mary, Birth-giver of God,
Whose flesh is God's at his creating word;
The second Eve, who heals the pain of Eve,
Whose Son has come to make the whole world new.

Your rule, O Christ our God, will last for ever,
Your coming has made light to shine on all;
You are the image of the Father's glory
Sprung from the Virgin's womb to save our race.

The Second Sunday of Christmas

Refrain:

Tone:

Verses:

When you were lifted high upon the cross
You raised up those who sat enchained in death;
For you alone are free of death's dominion:
O risen Saviour, source of light, have mercy!

The image of the Father, Christ our God
Assumes a servant's form yet changes not;
And from the Virgin Mother issues forth
To fill the world with God's eternal light.

True God he is, true God he will remain,
Yet takes upon himself what he was not;
And out of love for fallen humankind
Mortal becomes, to save mortality.

Our Saviour has appeared in human flesh
To fill the universe with holy light;
The shepherds see his glory and adore,
Wise men are guided by a star to Christ.

Lord Jesus, First-Begotten from the dead,
The first-fruits of God's harvesting to come,
You will return in glory as the Judge.
O risen Saviour, source of light, have mercy!

Epiphany

Refrain:

Let my prayer rise like in - - cense; my up-lift-ed hands as the eve-ning sac-ri - fice.

Tone:

Verses:

Today a star proclaims the Lord of light,
Heaven's brightness shines, for heaven is come to earth;
The Magi worship at their Maker's feet.
Glory to you, O Christ, our God, our light!

In gifts of gold and frankincense and myrrh
The King, the Priest, the Healer is revealed;
The High Priest and the Sacrifice are one.
Glory to you, O Christ, our God, our light!

The Light of the world for Baptism draws near,
The Holy Spirit as a dove descends,
The Father speaks, acclaiming his own Son,
Glory to you, O Christ, our God, our light!

A marriage feast is blessed, for Christ is present,
Water obeys the One who gave it form,
And, at his word, takes on the form of wine.
Glory to you, O Christ, our God, our light!

Blessed are you, our God made manifest!
Blessed are you, the Saviour now revealed!
Blessed are you, the Star of Jacob's line,
Glory to you, O Christ, our God, our light!

The Baptism of Christ

Refrain:

Let my prayer rise like in - - cense;
my up - lift - ed hands as the eve - ning sac - ri - fice.

Tone:

Verses:

The Light of the World for Baptism draws near,
The Baptist witnessed to the Light and said:
'Behold the Lamb of God who sets us free.'
Glory to you, O sinless Christ of God!

The streams of Jordan now receive their source,
The clay invokes the hand that gave it form,
Saying 'Of you should I now be baptized!'
Glory to you, the Maker, Christ our God!

The servant's hand baptizes Christ his Master,
The Holy Spirit like a dove descends,
The Father speaks, acclaiming his own Son.
Glory to you, the Saviour, Christ our God!

Though in the form of God, a servant's form
You took and in that form you were baptized
To glorify the flesh you had assumed.
Glory to you, O Christ, Incarnate Word!

Before the Forerunner you bowed your head
And crushed the heads of dragons in the deep;
You filled Creation's depths with saving light.
Glory to you, the Light, O Christ our God!

Prayer to conclude the Service of Incense

Advent and Christmas
Gracious God,
let our evening prayer rise before you,
and let our hands be uplifted
to welcome the coming of your Christ,
who is one with you and the Holy Spirit,
now and for ever.

Epiphany and the Baptism of Christ
In the gifts of the Magi, Lord God,
you disclose the mystery of your Christ
as King and God and healing sacrifice.
Let your Holy Spirit
lift up our hands in praise and prayer,
that we may become for you
a holy sacrifice acceptable in Christ,
who is one with you and the Holy Spirit,
now and for ever.

Evening Prayer may follow the services of Light and Incense. It should begin with the psalm or psalms appointed for the celebration.

The Vigil of Christmas

After the Service of Light (and Incense), the Vigil may continue with a pattern of readings, responsorial psalms and collects selected from these:

First Reading: Genesis 15:1–18
God promises Abraham a multitude of descendants.

Psalm 33

or: Genesis 18:1–15
God promises to Abraham that Sarah will bear him a son.

Psalm 33

Collect

God and Father of all believers,
you promised Abraham that his descendants
should be as many as the stars of heaven,
and in the coming of your Christ
you have brought that promise to fulfilment.
Grant us joy at his birth,
so that when he comes in glory
he may find us prepared and waiting,
faithful to his gospel
and exultant in his praises.
We ask this through Christ our Lord.

Second Reading: 2 Samuel 7:1–17
The prophet Nathan's words to King David.

Psalm 89:19–29

Collect

Eternal God,
who from the lineage of David
have raised up a temple for us
in the body of Jesus Christ, the Saviour,
show us your mercy
in this, your sacred place,
and make us obedient to your word,
that we may worship you in spirit and in truth.
We ask this through Christ our Lord.

Third Reading: Isaiah 11:1–11
The vision of peace and righteous judgement.

Psalm 85

Collect

Gracious God,
in your Incarnate Word
earth and heaven are one.
Let justice and peace
be joined together in his rule,
and all things reconciled in him,
who is alive, now and for ever.

Fourth Reading: Galatians 3:23 — 4:7
Saint Paul writes of God's adopted children in Christ.

Psalm 2

Collect

God of truth,
by the work of your Spirit
you baptize us in Christ
and make us heirs of your promise.
Through faith you justify us;
let faithful service distinguish us
as a people united and moved
by your unfailing grace.
We ask this through Christ our Lord.

The Fifth Reading may be a non-scriptural reading. A good selection may be found in Celebrating the Seasons *(Canterbury Press 1999) or other collections of readings, such as:* From the Fathers to the Churches *(Collins 1983) or* Christ our Light – Patristic Readings on Gospel Themes *(Exordium Books 1981), which follows the Roman Gospel Lectionary for Sundays and so, in great part, the* Common Worship *Sunday Lectionary.*

After this reading, the Gospel acclamation is sung, or a suitable hymn.

Acclamation

Revelation 22:17
V/. Alleluia, Alleluia, Alleluia.
R/. Alleluia, Alleluia, Alleluia.
V/. The Spirit and the Bride say 'Come!'
Let everyone who hears say 'Come, Lord Jesus!'
R/. Alleluia, Alleluia, Alleluia.

Gospel Reading: Matthew 1:1–25

The Vigil should conclude with the hymn Te Deum Laudamus *and the Collect for Christmas Eve on p. 24.*

The Vigil of the Epiphany

After the Service of Light (and Incense), the Vigil may continue with a pattern of readings, responsorial psalms and collects selected from these:

First Reading: Numbers 24:1–17
The prophecy of Balaam concerning Israel.

Psalm 8

Collect

God of wonders,
your light has shone among us
like a bright star of morning,
for Christ has come,
born of the Virgin Mother.

Let the light of faith
be kindled again in our hearts
and draw us evermore to seek his face.
We ask this through Christ our Lord.

Second Reading: Isaiah 62:1–12
The glorious destiny of Jerusalem.

Psalm 122

Collect

Eternal God,
you call your people
to walk as pilgrims in this passing world,
with eyes set on the new Jerusalem.
Go before us on our journey,
show us the way to holiness
and bring us to our journey's end in peace.
We ask this through Christ our Lord.

Third Reading: Malachi 3:1–4
The coming of God's messenger.

Psalm 113

Collect

God of wonders,
you revealed to the world
the coming of your chosen one,
the Word incarnate, your Only-Begotten Son.
Draw the hearts of nations and peoples
to follow the light of faith,
so that from the rising of the sun to its setting
a pure offering may be made to your glory.
We ask this through Christ our Lord.

Fourth Reading: Ephesians 1:3–14
God's purpose to unite all things together in Christ.

Psalm 148

Collect

God of light and vigour undying,
look with mercy on the whole Church,
your gift to us, a mystery and sacrament,
and in your eternal providence
complete the work of our redemption.
Let the whole world see and know
that what was fallen has been raised up,
that what was old is now made new,
and that all things are being restored to wholeness
in Christ himself,
through whom they had their origin,
who is alive for ever and ever.

The Fifth Reading may be a non-scriptural reading. A good selection may be found in Celebrating the Seasons *(Canterbury Press 1999) or other collections of readings, such as:* From the Fathers to the Churches *(Collins 1983) or* Christ our Light – Patristic Readings on Gospel Themes *(Exordium Books 1981), which follows the Roman Gospel Lectionary for Sundays and so, in great part, the* Common Worship *Sunday Lectionary.*

After this reading, the Gospel acclamation is sung, or a suitable hymn.

Acclamation

Revelation 22:17
V/. Alleluia, Alleluia, Alleluia.
R/. Alleluia, Alleluia, Alleluia.
V/. The Spirit and the Bride say 'Come!'

Let everyone who hears say 'Come, Lord Jesus!'
R/. Alleluia, Alleluia, Alleluia.

The Gospel for the Epiphany (Matthew 2:1–12) may be read. If another reading is chosen, it might be taken from the second or third service options for Epiphany: John 2:1–11 or John 1:29–34. Alternatively, the Christmas Gospel, John 1:1–18, might be read.

The Vigil should conclude with the hymn Te Deum Laudamus *and the Collect for the Eve of Epiphany on p. 37.*

The Vigil of the Baptism of Christ

After the Service of Light (and Incense), the Vigil may continue with a pattern of readings, responsorial psalms and collects selected from these:

First Reading: Exodus 3:1–15
Moses encounters 'The One who is'.

Psalm 99

Collect

Holy God,
whose name defies all speech,
grant that, as your likeness is revealed
in the face of Jesus your beloved,
so also your purposes may be manifest
in our obedience to the gospel of salvation.
We ask this through Christ our Lord.

Second Reading: Isaiah 44:1–6
God proclaims loyalty to his servant.

Psalm 20

Collect

Almighty God,
you revealed Jesus your servant
as your beloved Son,
anointed by the Holy Spirit.
Keep faith with us
who are your children in Christ,
and by the gifts of the Spirit
make us effective servants of your saving will.
We ask this through Christ our Lord.

Third Reading: Isaiah 62:1–12
God announces the nearness of salvation.

Psalm 147:13–21

Collect

God, whose word is nigh
and whose salvation is close at hand,
we pray you, take delight in your people
and see in us what you see in Christ,
that our joy may be full
and your purposes fulfilled.
We ask this through Christ our Lord.

Fourth Reading: Romans 6:1–11
We are baptized into the death of Christ.

Psalm 118:19–29

Collect

God, our true life,
let those you have baptized in Christ
be fashioned by your Spirit
into a new creation,

freed from sin
and living only for you.
We ask this through Christ our Lord.

The Fifth Reading may be a non-scriptural reading. A good selection may be found in Celebrating the Seasons *(Canterbury Press 1999) or other collections of readings, such as:* From the Fathers to the Churches *(Collins 1983) or* Christ our Light – Patristic Readings on Gospel Themes *(Exordium Books 1981), which follows the Roman Gospel Lectionary for Sundays and so, in great part, the* Common Worship *Sunday Lectionary.*

After this reading, the Gospel acclamation is sung, or a suitable hymn.

Acclamation

Luke 4:18
V/. Alleluia, Alleluia, Alleluia.
R/. Alleluia, Alleluia, Alleluia.
V/. The Spirit of the Lord is upon me,
because he has anointed me.
R/. Alleluia, Alleluia, Alleluia.

Gospel Reading: John 1:29–34

The Vigil should conclude with the hymn Te Deum Laudamus *and the Collect on p. 44.*

The Vigil Service for Sunday

If the Saturday Evening Vigil is a regular part of worship, then readings may be chosen on a 'continuous reading' basis from one of the available lectionaries.

Between the readings, canticles may be used (see the selection in Common Worship, Daily Prayer *(Church House Publishing 2002), pp. 493–575), followed by times of silence. If appropriate, the Scripture-related opening prayer for the Sunday or feast might be used after the responsorial canticle.*

A psalm or psalms may be recited before the readings, or between them as an alternative to canticles. If psalm prayers are desired, the psalms should be followed by a time of silence and the psalm prayer. Common Worship – Daily Prayer *has psalm prayers attached to the psalms in the Psalter, pp. 575ff. It is appropriate for people to sit for the psalms and prayers.*

The Taizé responses might be useful aids to prayer during the readings at the Vigil.

The readings should conclude with the Gospel of the coming Sunday, or of the festival, preceded by the acclamation Alleluia *with appropriate verse, or a suitable hymn.*

The outline of A Service of the Word *allows for a homily, but this is not necessary if a reading from the Patristic tradition appropriate to the Gospel has been chosen.*

Long readings may be read in short portions with silence between them rather than as one single extract.

The Conclusion of the Vigil

The Vigil may end with the hymn Te Deum Laudamus, *followed by the Collect of the Sunday, a blessing and dismissal.*

PART FOUR

PROPER TEXTS FOR THE WEEKDAYS OF ADVENT

The weekdays of Advent reflect the dual focus of the season. For the first three weeks, the emphasis is both on the Incarnation and on the Coming of Christ in Glory. On 17 December, for the week before Christmas, the focus shifts more to the celebration of Christ's birth.

For each day, a collect or opening prayer is given. The prayers at the preparation of the table and after Communion in the first part of the season are taken from the previous Sunday. For the last week, proper prayers are given throughout.

Prefaces are also given, a selection for the first part of Advent, then designated prefaces for the last week. If desired, the preface for the first Sunday may be used during the first three weeks, and that of the fourth Sunday during the last week.

Weekdays until 16 December

Monday

Opening prayers

Week 1
God, our hope,
make us eager to await
the advent of Christ your Son,
so that when he comes knocking,
he may find us vigilant in prayer
and exultant in your praise.

We make this prayer
through Jesus Christ, the Lord.

Week 2
Holy God,
let our prayer and petition
come before you,
so that with pure and undivided hearts
we may approach the great mystery
of Christ's Incarnation.
We make this prayer
through Jesus Christ, the Lord.

Week 3
God of compassion,
be attentive to our calling,
and with the grace of your Son who comes among us,
enlighten the darkness of our hearts.
We make this prayer
through Jesus Christ, the Lord.

Prayer over the Gifts
As for the First Sunday of Advent

Prayer after Communion
As for the First Sunday of Advent

Tuesday

Opening prayers

Week 1
God of mercy, we pray you,
listen to our prayer
and stand by us in all our trials.
Let the presence of your Son

free us from self-centredness
and the hope of his glorious return
fill us with longing to see him face to face.
We make this prayer
through Jesus Christ, the Lord.

Week 2
O God,
through the coming of Christ
you have made known your salvation.
Grant, we pray,
that we may prepare joyfully
for the glory of his birth.
We make this prayer
through Jesus Christ, the Lord.

Week 3
O God, who through your only Son
fashioned us to be a new creation,
look with kindness on this work of your mercy
and by the coming of Christ
remove from us all trace
of our old and sinful ways.
We make this prayer
through Jesus Christ, the Lord.

Prayer over the Gifts
As for the Second Sunday of Advent

Prayer after Communion
As for the Second Sunday of Advent

Wednesday

Opening prayers

Week 1
God, our salvation,
let your Holy Spirit prepare our hearts,
so that at the coming of Christ your Son
we may be found worthy to share
in the banquet of eternal life,
and to receive from his hands the food of heaven.
We make this prayer
through Jesus Christ, the Lord.

Week 2
God of wisdom,
whose word bids us prepare
the way for Christ the Lord,
grant in your kindness
that our weakness may never discourage us
as we long for him,
the healer of soul and body.
We make this prayer
through Jesus Christ, the Lord.

Week 3
Compassionate God,
grant that the coming feast of your Son
may impart healing to us in this present life
and bestow on us the blessings of the life to come.
We make this prayer
through Jesus Christ, the Lord.

Prayer over the Gifts
As for the Third Sunday of Advent

Prayer after Communion
As for the Third Sunday of Advent

Thursday

Opening prayers

Week 1
Lord, stir up your power
and support us with your great strength;
let your grace and mercy bring us quickly
the salvation that only our sins delay.
We make this prayer
through Jesus Christ, the Lord.

Week 2
Stir up our hearts, Lord,
to prepare the way for your Only-Begotten Son,
so that through his coming
we may be made ready to serve you
in freedom and singleness of heart.
We make this prayer
through Jesus Christ, the Lord.

Week 3
Gracious God,
bring joy to us,
through the coming of your Son,
and though of ourselves
we cannot claim to be righteous,
let Christ be our righteousness,
our freedom and our peace.
We ask this in his name,
Christ the Lord, now and for ever.

Prayer over the Gifts
As for the First Sunday of Advent

Prayer after Communion
As for the First Sunday of Advent

Friday

Opening prayers

Week 1
Jesus, our deliverer,
raise up your power and come;
protect us from the evil that threatens us
and set us free to receive your kingdom,
for you are alive, and reign,
now and for ever.

Week 2
Eternal God,
keep your people vigilant
as we await the return of your Only-Begotten Son,
that we may hasten with lighted lamps
to greet the author of our salvation.
We make this prayer
through Jesus Christ, the Lord.

Week 3
Almighty God,
let your grace go before us and follow us,
and as with heartfelt longing
we await the coming of your only Son,
let us receive your support in this present life
and the fullness of joy in the life to come.
We make this prayer
through Jesus Christ, the Lord.

Prayer over the Gifts
As for the Second Sunday of Advent

Prayer after Communion
As for the Second Sunday of Advent

Saturday

Opening prayers

Week 1
O God, you sent your only Son into this world
to free the human race from its ancient bondage.
As we watch for his coming, lavish upon us
your gifts and blessings from on high,
so that we may attain to the freedom
which you bestow on all your children.
We make this prayer
through Jesus Christ, the Lord.

Week 2
All-powerful God,
we pray that the splendour of your glory
may dawn in our hearts.
Let the advent of your Only-Begotten Son
scatter the darkness and reveal us
as children of the light.
We make this prayer
through Jesus Christ, the Lord.

Prayer over the Gifts
As for the Third Sunday of Advent

Prayer after Communion
As for the Third Sunday of Advent

Eucharistic Preface

*For Weekday celebrations of the Eucharist in the first part of
Advent, the preface of the previous Sunday may be used, or one
of these shorter prefaces.*

The light of Christ
It is indeed right for us to give you thanks,
God most high and holy,
through your Son, Jesus Christ.

By the advent of his light
he scattered the darkness of this world
and revealed to us the way
by which we may find eternal life.

And so with all creation,
we give you glory and say: Holy . . .

Joy and peace in Christ's coming
Worthy are you, our God,
of glory, thanksgiving and praise,
through Jesus Christ, your Son.

From his fullness
Christ has bestowed joy and peace on all
and by the splendour of his truth
has brought salvation.

Therefore, with all the powers of heaven,
we glorify your holy name: Holy . . .

Christ – our reconciliation and salvation
It is indeed right for us to give you thanks,
God most high and holy,
through your Son, Jesus Christ.

Through the advent of Christ
you have reconciled humankind to yourself
and in the life of Christ
you have shown us your salvation.

And so we name you
the worker of wonders
as we joyfully acclaim: Holy . . .

The Advent pilgrimage
It is truly right and just
for us to give you thanks, O God,
through Jesus Christ your Son.

Rejoicing in faith and hope
your Church hastens on its pilgrim way
to greet the advent of Christ,
until, in the fullness of your kingdom,
your people enter with their Master
into the eternal wedding feast.

And so, with angels and saints,
we glorify your holy name: Holy . . .

Weekdays between 17 and 24 December

17 December

Opening prayer

Creator God, redeemer of humankind,
you ordained that your Word should take flesh
in the womb of the Virgin Mary.
Look with kindness on our prayers,
so that your Son, who is one with us in our humanity,
may make us one with him in your divine life
where he is glorified
now and for ever.

Prayer over the Gifts

We prepare your table, Lord,
with bread and wine that earth has given
and human hands have made.
Through these holy mysteries,
renew us with the food and drink of heaven.
We ask this through Christ, the Lord.

Eucharistic Preface

We lift our hearts to you,
God eternal, true and faithful.
To you we offer thanks and praise
through Jesus Christ your Son.

Though he is God,
he came to us in the lowliness of human flesh,
so that he might free from death
those he had called to inherit eternal life;
and he is to return in glory
to bestow the fullness of the kingdom
on those he has redeemed.

And so, with angels and all saints,
we glorify your holy name: Holy . . .

or:

It is truly right and just, our duty and our salvation,
always and everywhere to give you thanks,
Lord, holy Father, almighty and eternal God.

Because from a human birth
the Creator of all things is to be born,
and that which was lost to us in Adam
is now restored in Christ.

And so, with the angels we give you glory
in this, their joyful hymn of praise: Holy . . .

Prayer after Communion

God, our provider,
we bless you for this food of life.
Enkindle us by your Spirit,
that we may shine like bright lamps
before the face of Christ at his coming.
We ask this through Christ, the Lord.

18 December

Opening prayer

God, whose will is our freedom,
grant that we who labour under the yoke
of ancient slavery to sin
may be set free by the longed-for new birth
of your Only-Begotten Son.
We make this prayer
through Jesus Christ our Lord.

Prayer over the Gifts

Joyous God,
let the offering of praise and thanksgiving
glorify your name and bring us closer to you,
that we may come to share in the undying life of Christ
who healed our mortal nature by assuming our mortality.
We ask this through Christ our Lord.

Eucharistic Preface

Worthy are you, our God,
of glory, thanksgiving and praise,
through Jesus Christ, your Son.

At his first coming
he restored us to your friendship
and at his return he has promised
to bestow a kingdom on his faithful people
in the company of the angels.

With them we bless your name
and join their exultant hymn of praise: Holy . . .

Prayer after Communion

Gracious God,
let us receive your mercy
in the midst of your temple
and with fitting acts of reverence
look forward to the feast of our redemption.
We ask this through Jesus Christ, the Lord.

19 December

Opening prayer

Almighty God,
whose glory has been revealed
through the childbearing of the Virgin Mary,
grant, we pray,
that we may worship in faith
and celebrate with reverence
the mystery of this wondrous Incarnation.
We make this prayer
through Jesus Christ our Lord.

Prayer over the Gifts

Lord, regard us with kindness
as we place these gifts on your table,
so that what is prepared in weakness
may be made a source of strength for us.
We ask this through Christ our Lord.

Eucharistic Preface

We lift our hearts to you,
the one eternal God,
and give you thanks and praise.

Your mercy has come down from on high,
the Saviour is revealed in human form
and earth, the home of mortals,
receives its Maker and its King.

And so we praise you,
joining angels and archangels
in their exultant shout of praise: Holy . . .

Prayer after Communion

All-powerful God,
as we give thanks for your gifts,
make us long for what is to come,
so that we may welcome the birth of our Saviour
and honour it with purity of heart.
We ask this through Christ our Lord.

20 December

Opening prayer

God, by whose gracious plan
the Virgin Mary conceived your Word
at the message of the angel
and, filled with the light of the Holy Spirit,
became the dwelling of your Godhead;
grant that, through her example,
we may live and work in faithfulness
to your purpose of salvation.
We make this prayer
through Jesus Christ our Lord.

Prayer over the Gifts

As we come before you, Lord God,
we pray that through our sharing in this mystery

we may receive those blessings
which we await in hope and faith.
We ask this through Christ our Lord.

Eucharistic Preface

It is truly right to give you thanks,
holy Father, eternal God.

You sent your Word to become incarnate
in the womb of the Virgin Mary,
so that, in sharing our human nature,
he might gather us to himself
as heirs to the divine life.

And so, with angels and saints,
we glorify your holy name: Holy . . .

Prayer after Communion

Keep watch, Lord, and protect
those whom you refresh with your gift from heaven;
and let your peace bring joy
to those who are blessed by these holy mysteries.
We ask this through Christ our Lord.

21 December

Opening prayer

God of mercy, listen, we pray,
to the prayers of your people,
so that as we rejoice
at the coming of your Only-Begotten Son
in this human body,
we may receive the blessing of eternal life
when he comes again in glory.

We make this prayer
through Jesus Christ our Lord.

Prayer over the Gifts

Lord, bless what we set on your table,
for these are your gifts to us,
and by your power you transform them
into the sacrament of our salvation.
We ask this through Jesus Christ our Lord.

Eucharistic Preface

Worthy are you, our God,
of glory, thanksgiving and praise,
through Jesus Christ, your Son.

As we prepare for his birthday,
we recall with joy his first coming
and turn in hope and expectation
to his return in glory.

Therefore, with all the powers of heaven,
we glorify your holy name: Holy . . .

Prayer after Communion

Lord, let our part in this divine mystery
be for your people a source of strength,
and as we serve your glory
bring us in mind and body
to the fullness of salvation.
We ask this through Christ our Lord.

22 December

Opening prayer

Compassionate God,
you saw our human race lie victim to death
and in your love you formed the plan of our salvation
through the coming of your Only-Begotten Son.
Grant that as we celebrate his Incarnation,
so we may be found worthy of a place
in the company of those he has redeemed.
We make this prayer
through Jesus Christ our Lord.

Prayer over the Gifts

Trusting in your loving mercy, Lord,
we hasten with gifts to prepare your holy altar;
let your grace make us holy
through the very mysteries
by which we serve your glory.
We ask this through Christ our Lord.

Eucharistic Preface

It is truly right and just to tell of the wonders
which you, our God, have worked for your people,
and in the song of the Virgin Mary
to glorify your steadfast love.

Truly you have looked with favour
on the lowly and poor;
and fulfilled your promise of mercy
by giving us, through Mary,
your Christ, the author of our salvation.

Therefore we praise you
and name you the Holy One, as we say: Holy . . .

Prayer after Communion

Lord, let your sacrament strengthen us,
so that when the Saviour comes,
we may be ready to meet him
with deeds worthy of his name
and receive his eternal blessing.
We ask this through Christ our Lord.

23 December

Opening prayer

Almighty and eternal God,
the birth of your Son is drawing near.
We pray that your Word
may show your glory
to us, your unworthy servants,
since it was your purpose
that he should become incarnate of the Virgin Mary
and pitch his tent among us:
for he is one with you and the Holy Spirit,
now and for ever.

Prayer over the Gifts

Lord,
by Christ's offering of himself
you have given us the pattern of all worship.
Let Christ also be the source
of perfect reconciliation,
to cleanse us in mind and heart
as we await his holy birth.
We ask this through Jesus Christ our Lord.

Eucharistic Preface

Worthy are you, our God,
of glory, thanksgiving and praise,
through Jesus Christ, your Son.

At his first coming he restored us to your friendship
and at his return he has promised
to bestow a kingdom on his faithful people
in the company of the angels.

With them we bless your name
and join their exultant hymn: Holy . . .

Prayer after Communion

Grant your peace, Lord,
to those you have fed with gifts from heaven,
so that, with lamps burning, we may be worthy
to meet your beloved Son at his coming.
We ask this through Christ our Lord.

24 December – Christmas Eve, in the morning

Opening prayer

Come quickly, we beg you:
Lord Jesus, do not delay,
and by your gracious advent
uplift and console
those who long for your appearing.
For yours is the glory,
with the Father and the Holy Spirit,
now and for ever.

Prayer over the Gifts

Lord, accept our praise and service,
that this holy feast may free us from sin
and prepare us in heart and mind
to greet the glory of your Son's birth.
We ask this through Jesus Christ our Lord.

Eucharistic Preface

It is truly right and just, our duty and our salvation,
to give you thanks, most gracious God,
and speak your praises with exultant heart.

Our redemption is drawing near,
the promise made to our ancestors
is about to be fulfilled,
and the one who comes in lowly birth
is welcomed already as the life-giving Lord.

Therefore with angels and saints
we sing the unending hymn of your glory: Holy . . .

Prayer after Communion

Lord, we are refreshed by your wonderful gift.
As we prepare to adore your Son in his earthly appearing,
grant us the joy and gladness of his blessing.
We ask this through Jesus Christ our Lord.

PART FIVE

PROPER TEXTS FOR THE
WEEKDAYS OF CHRISTMAS

The prayers given in this section may be used at a daily Eucharist
on weekdays of the period between Christmas and the Baptism
of Christ. The opening prayers may be used as collects for the
day at Morning or Evening Prayer.

The celebration of Epiphany marks the turning point of the
Christmas Season and the texts given here reflect the change in
emphasis that accompanies the Epiphany.

A selection of Christmas and Epiphany prefaces is also given
for optional use at the Eucharist on these days.

*The prayers for the feasts of Saint Stephen, Saint John the
Evangelist and the Holy Innocents are to be found on pp. 142–9*

29 December – the fifth day in the Christmas Octave

Opening prayer

Almighty God,
who banished the darkness of the world
by the coming of the true Light,
enlighten and inspire our hearts
to give you worthy praise
for the nativity of your Only-Begotten Son.
We make this prayer through Jesus Christ our Lord.

Prayer over the Gifts

God, our joy,
let praise and thanksgiving
be our offering today,
and as your eternal Word
takes on our human nature,
so in this holy exchange
may we be taken up into the likeness of Christ,
who is alive, now and for ever.

Prayer after Communion

Eternal God,
grant, we pray,
that our life may ever be sustained
by the power of these holy mysteries.
We ask this through Christ our Lord.

30 December

Opening prayer

God of wonders,
you have given us your Son,
incarnate of the Virgin, yet one with you in Godhead.
Let this new marvel of his human birth
free us from the ancient yoke of sin.
We make this prayer through Jesus Christ our Lord.

Prayer over the Gifts

With faith and joy, Lord,
we prepare the table of Christ.
By this holy meal,
unite us to his self-offering.
We ask this through Christ our Lord.

Prayer after Communion

God, our true life,
in this holy feast
you draw us close to yourself.
Let these holy things work in our hearts
to prepare us for the fullness of what you promise.
We ask this through Christ our Lord.

31 December

Opening prayer

Almighty and eternal God,
in the birth of your Son
you lay the foundation of our Christian faith.
Sustain us as his disciples,
and grant that we may always abide in him,
in whom is the fullness of life.
For he lives and reigns, now and for ever.

Prayer over the Gifts

Lord, open our lips
in praise and thanksgiving,
and as we prepare your table,
prepare our hearts and our lives
to give you glory.
We ask this through Christ our Lord.

Prayer after Communion

God, whose watchful care
upholds and embraces us always,
let these holy gifts be our support in this passing age,
that we may set our hearts on the joy of life eternal.
We ask this through Christ our Lord.

For 1 January, the Circumcision, see pp. 149–51.

Prayers for the weekdays between 1 January and the Baptism of Christ

Monday

Opening prayer

Before Epiphany
Gracious God,
you gave your Son
who is one with you in glory,
to share our humanity
and to be born of the Virgin Mother.
Keep us true to faith in Christ,
free us from evil
and bring us to eternal life.
We make this prayer through Jesus Christ our Lord.

After Epiphany
We pray you, Lord,
let your glory be our light.
Guide us through the darkness of this world
to the eternal radiance of our true native land.
We make this prayer through Jesus Christ our Lord.

Prayer over the Gifts

God of blessings,
bless us in preparing these gifts,
that we may be filled with the gift of your life.
We ask this through Christ our Lord.

Prayer after Communion

God, our provider,
sustain us by this sacred feast,
and day by day renew us
by the power of this holy sacrament.
We ask this through Christ our Lord.

Tuesday

Opening prayer

Before Epiphany
All-holy God,
you chose that your Son
should be born of the holy Virgin
and become like us in all things but sin.
Grant that we,
fashioned into a new creation in Christ,
may be set free from the deceits and snares of sin.
We make this prayer through Christ our Lord.

After Epiphany
God, whose Only-Begotten Son
has appeared in the substance of our flesh,
grant, we pray,
that acknowledging him outwardly
as one like ourselves,
we may be inwardly created anew.
We make this prayer through Jesus Christ our Lord.

Prayer over the Gifts

Gracious God,
welcome us as we set your table
and lead us more deeply into the mystery
which we profess in our thanksgiving.
We ask this through Christ our Lord.

Prayer after Communion

You touch our lives, O God,
as we share in this sacrament.
Let it so fashion our hearts
as to make us worthy of what we receive.
We ask this through Christ our Lord.

Wednesday

Opening prayer

Before Epiphany
Eternal God,
by a new light in the heavens
you announced to the world
the coming of salvation.
Let the light of Christ rise in our hearts
to make us a new creation in him.
We make this prayer through Jesus Christ our Lord.

After Epiphany
God, light of all nations,
bestow your peace, let earth rejoice,
and as you gave joy to your people
in the revelation of your Christ,
so let that joy be ours as we celebrate once again
the wonder of his appearing in our midst.
We make this prayer through Jesus Christ our Lord.

Prayer over the Gifts

God of peace,
source of true worship,
open our lips to praise your glory
and by the sacrifice of thanksgiving
draw us together into unity.
We ask this through Christ our Lord.

Prayer after Communion

God, our help,
in countless ways
you provide for your people.
Protect us now and always
that, reassured by your constant care,

we may make our way in trust and hope
along the path to eternal life.
We ask this through Christ our Lord.

Thursday

Opening prayer

Before Epiphany
God our Saviour,
with the birth of Christ your Son
you began the wonderful work of redemption.
Make our faith strong
so that guided by his Gospel
we may reach the glorious reward you promise.
We make this prayer through Jesus Christ our Lord.

After Epiphany
God, who through your Son
raised up the light of eternity for all nations,
grant that your people may acknowledge
the full splendour of their Redeemer,
so that by his grace they may enter into light everlasting.
We make this prayer through Jesus Christ our Lord.

Prayer over the Gifts

Bless us, Lord,
as we recall the birth of your Son
in thanksgiving and praise,
for by his coming he shows us the way of truth
and promises us the true life of your kingdom.
We ask this through Christ our Lord.

Prayer after Communion

Almighty God,
let this holy feast
rid us of all that is evil
and fulfil the good intentions
you put in our hearts.
We ask this through Christ our Lord.

Friday

Opening prayer

Before Epiphany
God, our light,
shine upon us
and set our hearts afire with your grace,
that we may always acknowledge Christ as the Saviour
and hold fast to the truth of his teaching.
We make this prayer through Jesus Christ our Lord.

After Epiphany
Grant, we pray, almighty God,
that the nativity of the Saviour,
made manifest by the star,
may be revealed in all its glory to us,
and grow more fully in our minds and hearts.
We make this prayer through Jesus Christ our Lord.

Prayer over the Gifts

Eternal God,
in the Word made Flesh
you brought heaven and earth into one
and made the whole creation holy.
Keep us holy as we offer praise to you.
We ask this through Christ our Lord.

Prayer after Communion

God, revealer of mysteries,
you have shown us your Christ
as your light and glory.
Send us forth now to serve him
in our brothers and sisters.
We ask this through Christ our Lord.

Saturday

Opening prayer

Before Epiphany
Creator God,
through the birth of your Only-Begotten Son
you filled the creation with new light.
Make us one with him
as he has become one with us
through his human birth of the Virgin Mary,
so that we may live joyfully
under the rule of your grace.
We make this prayer through Jesus Christ our Lord.

After Epiphany
God, holy and mighty,
who through your Only-Begotten Son
have made us a new creation,
grant, we pray, that by your grace
we may be found in his likeness
in whom our nature is united to you.
We make this prayer through Jesus Christ our Lord.

Eucharistic Prefaces

Christmas Season until Epiphany

Christ's birth, our new birth
It is truly right and just, our duty and our salvation,
always and everywhere to give you thanks,
Lord, holy Father, almighty and eternal God.

In the human birth of your eternal Son
you promise the new birth of humankind,
and through his blood shed upon the cross
you have brought redemption to all.

And so, with angels and all saints,
we exult and glorify your holy name: Holy . . .

Christ the true Light
It is truly right and just, our duty and our salvation,
always and everywhere to give you thanks,
Lord, holy Father, almighty and eternal God.

You have shown us the birth of the true light
which no darkness can overcome,
the light of Christ which rises in glory
for the salvation of the human race.

And so, with all the powers of heaven,
we glorify your holy name: Holy . . .

Christ, the medicine of immortality
We lift our hearts to you,
God eternal, true and faithful.
To you we offer thanks and praise
in the name of Jesus Christ your Son.

You have prepared a healing remedy
for the frailty of our mortal state,
as from a race in thrall to death
there rises a child whom death cannot overcome.

And so, with the song of all creation,
we glorify your holy name: Holy . . .

After Epiphany

The holy exchange
It is truly right and just, our duty and our salvation,
to give you thanks, almighty Father,
for you have revealed the One
who is the sacrament of salvation
and the light of nations.

In Christ your Son we know both God and Man
who with the fire of love and grace
assumed that human nature which is ours
to make us partakers of that Godhead which is his.

And so, with angels and all saints,
we exult and glorify your holy name: Holy . . .

The Fall undone
It is truly right and just, our duty and our salvation,
always and everywhere to give you thanks,
Lord, holy Father, almighty and eternal God.

From your presence we had been exiled
through the transgression of our first parents,
but now in compassion and mercy
you have called us to forgiveness and life
by sending your Son, our Saviour.

Through Christ the angels adore your glory
in this holy triumphal hymn: Holy . . .

PART SIX

TEXTS FOR SPECIAL
SERVICES OF ADVENT

Many churches hold special services during Advent and at Christmas. Often these have a popular character, with a particular emphasis on the participation of children. In this section, suggested outlines are given for the blessing of an Advent wreath, for an Advent carol service, a Christingle service, a setting of the Advent 'O' antiphons and a service of reconciliation for Advent.

The Blessing of the Advent Wreath

Greenery was at one time a common means of decorating public buildings and homes for Christmas. The Advent wreath seems to have made the transition from a domestic to a liturgical ornament, as many churches now use such a wreath at services. There are a variety of customs for making and decorating the wreath. What follows appears to be a popular usage.

The Advent wreath is primarily a visual object. It should therefore be significant in size. It should be made of evergreen branches woven into a circle. Four candles are placed in holders in the wreath. The candles are usually coloured, though the colours vary. Red is a common choice, though sometimes blue or violet candles are preferred, using the standard liturgical colours of Advent. In the middle of the wreath may be placed a white candle. The first candle is lit on the First Sunday of Advent, then two on the Second Sunday and so on. The centre candle is either lit from the beginning of Advent or at Christmas. The centre candle might also be placed and lit next to the Christmas Crib.

There is no set 'story' attached to the wreath and so preparing it is an opportunity for the creative imagination. As a circular object, it is a token of eternity, an idea with which the use of evergreens will also fit. It is sometimes said that the candles may represent the people who appear in the Scripture readings particularly associated with Advent: the prophets (Isaiah in particular) who foretold the Messiah; David, Christ's royal ancestor; John the Baptist; and the Blessed Virgin Mary. The centre candle, if used, would then represent Christ, the Light of the world. If the centre candle is lit from the beginning of Advent, it may signify Christ the ever-burning light; if at the conclusion of Advent, it may signify Christ the light who comes into the world at Christmas. Such identification of the candles would be a good way to draw attention to the themes of the Sundays of Advent.

If the wreath is sufficiently large so that larger candles are used, signs suggestive of these figures might be painted on or applied to the candles: perhaps a scroll for Isaiah, a crown and/or star for King David, the Lamb of God carrying a standard for Saint John the Baptist, a crowned lily for the Blessed Virgin Mary, a cross for Christ, and so on.

The wreath may be blessed and lit on the Sundays of Advent as part of the service, preferably at the beginning. The wreath may be carried in during the entrance procession. When the candles are lit, a prayer may be said. One of the Scripture-related opening prayers appropriate to the Sunday might be used or adapted. The prayers suggested below are slightly simpler and might be suitable for use with children. They might be chosen when the Sunday readings focus on or mention the figures mentioned above.

If a song is required for the blessing of the wreath, a suitable song, especially for children, might be a single verse of the hymn 'Long ago, prophets knew' (*New English Hymnal* 10). Verse 1 will suit the theme of the Prophets, verse 2 might be used for David, verse 4 for Mary. Verse 3 of the song 'The King of glory comes' (*Laudate* 107) mentions King David.

A prayer of blessing

True light of the World,
our Saviour Jesus Christ,
be blessed in these lights we kindle
to announce your advent among us.
Come as our teacher,
come as our peacemaker,
come to us and bring us your light;
Jesus, be blessed both now and for ever:
All: Amen.

*These short prayers of blessing may be used, Sunday by Sunday,
as appropriate:*

Isaiah and the prophets

Jesus, light of the world,
before you came to us
the prophets told of you,
that you would be the Prince of Peace.
Make peace for us
and make us peaceful.
Amen.

King David

Jesus, light of the world,
you come from the family of David,
the ancient king of your people.
Be our king too:
a king who is fair,
a king who is peaceful.
Amen.

John the Baptist

Jesus, light of the world,
John the Baptist spoke of you
as 'The One who is to come'.

Come to us, make us good,
make us ready to welcome you
at Christmastime.
Amen.

The Virgin Mary
Jesus, light of the world,
Mary became your mother
when she said 'Yes' to God's messenger.
Christmas is near;
make us ready to say 'yes'
to whatever you ask us to do.
Amen.

An Advent Carol Service

In many churches it is customary to hold a special service to mark the beginning of Advent. This is often modelled on the Christmas 'Nine Lessons' pattern. If held in the evening, the service might begin with a Service of Light (see pp. 47–50), or the blessing of the Advent wreath or a processional hymn.

The one who leads the service will then open the service with words such as these:

Dear friends in Christ,
as Advent begins,
let us take time to reflect
on the coming of Christ.

We have known this coming
in the holy birth at Bethlehem.
We experience this coming
in the hearing of the word
and in the fellowship of Christ's table.
We look for this coming
and the promised resurrection of the dead.

Advent

In these days of preparation
let us turn our hearts and minds
to the One whose presence among us
is to be so gloriously made manifest.
May he bring us to know more deeply
the meaning of this season,
so that we may celebrate his birth
as our brother and our master,
in whom we have been made the children of God.

or:

Dear friends in Christ,
with joyful expectation
we are preparing to celebrate the human birth
of God's all-creating Word.
We pray that as we rejoice
to receive him as Redeemer,
so we may face him with confidence and hope
when he comes as the judge of all.

In order that we may draw more deeply
on the meaning of this wonderful season,
let us listen to the Advent voice:
the voice of the Prophet
calling the people to prepare the way of the Lord;
the voice of John the Baptist
announcing the One who is to come;
the voice of Mary,
pledging herself as the servant of God's purpose.

May Christ find us
keeping joyful vigil for his return.
May he make us new in faith,
joyful in hope
and quick to do the works of love
in which he presents himself to us.

Some of the following readings may be chosen. Between the readings, suitable Advent carols or hymns should be sung by the congregation or performed by the choir.

Isaiah 2:10–17 The Lord alone shall be exalted in that day.

Isaiah 11:1–9 They will not hurt or destroy on all my holy mountain.

Isaiah 25:6–10 Lo, this is our God. Let us rejoice in his salvation.

Isaiah 35:1–10 Here is your God.

Isaiah 40:1–5 Prepare the way of the Lord.

Matthew 3:1–11 The appearance of John the Baptist.

Mark 1:1–8 The appearance of John the Baptist.

Luke 3:1–14 The teaching of John the Baptist.

Luke 1:26–38 The Annunciation to the Blessed Virgin Mary.

Non-scriptural readings are also appropriate. Good collections of non-scriptural readings both ancient and modern that follow the liturgical outline of Advent may be found in Celebrating the Seasons *(Canterbury Press 2002). Many Advent and Christmas anthologies will also provide ideas.*

Instead of a 'Bidding Prayer' at the opening of the service, it would be more appropriate to the natural patterns of the Liturgy of the Word if the service were to conclude with intercessions in the form of short biddings such as the following:

Advent

Leader:
In joyful expectation of his coming,
let us pray to Christ, the Lord:

All: Come, Lord Jesus!

Christ, anointed of God,
whose coming was foretold by the prophets,
come to us as the Prince of Peace:

All: Come, Lord Jesus!

Son of the Most High,
announced by the Angel to the Blessed Virgin Mary,
come to rule over your people for ever:

All: Come, Lord Jesus!

Holy One of God,
greeted and acclaimed by John the Baptist,
come to the earth in joy and judgement:

All: Come, Lord Jesus!

Light of the world,
light that darkness cannot quench,
come and open our eyes to your glory:

All: Come, Lord Jesus!

Remember us, Lord, when you come into your kingdom
and teach us to pray:

The Lord's Prayer is said.

The service may conclude with the collect for the first Sunday of Advent, or with one of the Scripture-related opening prayers in Part 1.

The Christingle Service

For hundreds of years in northern Europe both before and after the Reformation, Christmas Eve was the occasion for colourful services and processions. Popular songs such as the 'carol' we now sing as *In dulci iubilo* ('Good Christian men, rejoice!') formed part of these services. Lighted torches or candles were distributed for the processions.

At Marienborn in Germany, a few days before Christmas in the year 1747, the Moravian congregation held a Christmas service for the children of the community. The leader of the service, John de Watteville, retold the Christmas story, then gave to each child a lighted candle tied with a red ribbon. He prayed that Christ would kindle a flame in their hearts, 'that theirs like thine become'. The community records state that the children were greatly pleased by this idea. It soon took root among the members of the Moravian Church, and as their members emigrated the tradition of the Christmas candle spread wherever they went. The name 'Christingle' became attached to the candles, and then to the whole service. Moravians usually celebrate Christingle on the Sunday before Christmas or on Christmas Eve.

Some forty years ago the Christingle Service was introduced into Great Britain by The Children's Society as a way of generating support for its work. The service has become popular with churches and schools as a part of their preparation for Christmas.

The 'Christingle' candle itself has undergone some elaboration in its history. Nowadays it usually takes the form of an orange, in which a hole is made to insert a small candle. Cocktail sticks are inserted into the orange, on which are impaled dried fruit. The orange is tied with a red ribbon. The service is a celebration of the birth of Jesus that brings light to the whole world.

The origins and meaning of the Christingle itself are lost. Nowadays, the term is usually interpreted as 'Christ light'. The orange represents the world, the candle, Christ the Light of the world, the dried fruits, the fruits of the earth. The ribbon's red colour is supposed to be a reminder of the blood of Christ and the salvation of the world. The outline service given here takes up those themes as its main focus.

If it is possible, this service will require the creation of a sizeable globe of coloured paper and the various elements that make up the Christingle. Baskets of fruit will be needed, and a piece of red ribbon long enough to tie around the globe. A candle will need to stand above the globe or in front of it. The small orange christingles will also be prepared on trays for distribution to the congregation. Given the origins of the service, children should play prominent parts in it. Action should predominate over words.

Appropriate hymns or songs may be sung while the congregation gathers.

The leader greets the people:

Leader: In darkness, let there be light:
All: Jesus Christ, the light of the world.

The leader welcomes the congregation and as part of an introduction to the service may use words like these:

We come together to celebrate Jesus, the light of the world.
We listen to the word of God:
telling us how the universe was made,
how the earth brought forth its fruit,
and how, in the fullness of time,
God sent Jesus Christ to save us by his blood.

The appropriate number of candles on the Advent wreath may be lit and a suitable song sung. A time of quiet may be kept.

A reader reads Genesis 1:1–5, 31.

Leader: God gave us the world.
All: We live together in God's world.

A suitable song is sung. If it is possible to carry the large globe in, it is placed in front or in the midst of the congregation.

A reader reads Genesis 1:29.

Leader: God gave us the fruits of the earth,
All: for us to share and praise God's name.

Children place the baskets of fruit around the globe as a suitable song is sung.

A reader reads 1 Peter 1:18–21.

Leader: Christ's lifeblood is our life.
All: Jesus shed his blood for the life of the world.

Children tie the length of red ribbon round the large globe while a suitable song is sung.

A reader reads John 8:12.

Leader: Jesus Christ is the light of the world:
All: The darkness cannot overcome the light of Christ.

A child lights the candle by the globe while a suitable song is sung. The congregation is invited to keep a short time of silence.

The leader may give a short address on the Christingle.

A suitable song may be sung. If a collection of money or goods is to be taken for charity it should be done here.

The christingles are distributed. The leader says:

Everything comes from God:
the world and all that is in it,
the fruits of the earth to feed us,

the blood of Jesus which has saved us,
the light of Jesus to light our way.

Take one of these lights,
give it to the person next to you.
Be light for the world.

Suitable music or songs should accompany the distribution. The congregation pass the christingles to each other. Everyone should receive one from someone else. The congregation light the candles and pass the light around the church. When all are standing with their candles lit, the leader invites the congregation to pray.

Short prayers such as these should be offered, particularly for the world and for those nations and peoples in need:

Leader: Let us remember God's world:

All: You gave us this wonderful world.
Bless us and make us care for your gift.

Let us remember all the people in God's world:

All: You have made all men and women as one family.
Bless us and help us care for each other.

Let us remember those in need:

All: You want everyone to be free from poverty.
Make us generous with all the good things we enjoy.

Let us remember all children:

All: Keep them safe.
Help them grow in your love.

Responses, such as Taizé chants, may be sung during the prayers.

Texts for Special Services

The prayers should conclude with the Lord's Prayer.

The service ends with the following:

Leader: We have shared with each other the light of Christ:
All: God make us into lights for the world.
Leader: We want to share with each other the fruits of the earth:
All: God grant that we may bear the fruits of the Spirit.
Leader: May the peace of Christ be with us always.
All: God give us peace, and peace for all the world.

or this final prayer:

God, our light,
open the eyes of everyone
to the goodness of your creation,
to the blessings of earth's produce
and to the truth of Jesus Christ.
Bind us together
in the communion of his blood
and the fellowship of the Holy Spirit.
We ask this in the name of Jesus,
who is one with you and the Holy Spirit,
now and for ever.

All: Amen.

The leader says: Go now, in the peace of Christ.
All: Thanks be to God.

A suitable song is sung to end the service.

The Advent 'O' Antiphons

The Advent 'O' Antiphons are a collection of seven anthems addressed to Christ, so called because each one begins with the address: *O Wisdom*; *O Adonai*, etc. They name Christ as Lord by applying to him some of the divine or royal titles that are found in the Old Testament. In form they are Advent prayers for deliverance, each one ending with the invocation *Veni* – Come!

From medieval times in the rites of the Roman tradition these antiphons were sung at Vespers or Evensong in conjunction with the song of the Blessed Virgin Mary, the Magnificat, during the week before Christmas. In the Roman Liturgy they were assigned to 17–23 December, whereas the daily service of medieval England arranged their recitation to begin one day earlier on the 16th, since a further anthem, addressed to the Blessed Virgin Mary, was assigned to 23 December. In the *Book of Common Prayer* calendar, the opening words of the first Antiphon 'O Sapientia' are still found entered for 16 December.

In recent years the Antiphons have become popular with choirs to sing at Evensong, owing perhaps to their particularly striking melody. A number of translations are in use, of which the best known is probably that in the *New English Hymnal*, no. 503.

The Advent Antiphons are perhaps better known under the disguise of a metrical paraphrase. This is the famous Advent hymn 'O come, O come, Emmanuel', which seems to have originated as a Latin composition in Franciscan circles at the beginning of the eighteenth century.

Like many lyrical liturgical texts, the Antiphons are best chanted or sung. To help those who might like to use them but would prefer a metrical melody for the antiphon with a simple chant tone for the verses of the canticle, here is a setting of the Magnificat that employs the Antiphons in metrical form to be sung to the melody of 'O come, O come, Emmanuel'.

On each day, the appropriate four-line antiphon, together with its chorus, should be sung in full before and after the Magnificat. Between each verse of the canticle the chorus

'Rejoice, rejoice' should be sung. This chorus echoes Saint Paul's words in a popular traditional New Testament reading for Advent from Philippians 4:4 – *Rejoice in the Lord always; I say again, rejoice.* The words are a particularly appropriate refrain to the Magnificat in view of the traditional identification of the Blessed Virgin Mary as personifying the 'Daughter of Israel' portrayed in such texts as Zephaniah 3:14ff.

I have used the older second person singular forms of address in these antiphons, so that there will be correspondence with the Prayer Book text of the Magnificat. It would be easy to substitute the modern equivalents when a modern text of the canticle is used.

17 December

Come, holy Wisdom, breath of God,
The Father's all-fulfilling Word,
Creator Wisdom, strength and stay,
Teach us to walk thy royal way.
Rejoice! Rejoice! Emmanuel
Shall come to thee, O Israel.

18 December

O come, O come, Adonai,
Who in a blaze of majesty
To Moses came and spoke the Law
On Sinai's height in fear and awe.
Rejoice! Rejoice! Emmanuel
Shall come to thee, O Israel.

19 December

O come, thou root of Jesse's tree,
Who stand for all the world to see;
Let nations seek thy gentle sway,
O come to us without delay!

Rejoice! Rejoice! Emmanuel
Shall come to thee, O Israel.

20 December

O key of royal David, come!
Unlock the doors of heaven's home.
What thou hast opened, none shall close,
Safeguard for us the heavenward road.
Rejoice! Rejoice! Emmanuel
Shall come to thee, O Israel.

21 December

O Come, bright Star of morning skies,
O Sun of justice, now arise!
Make radiant with thy holy light
The prisoners held in death's dark night.
Rejoice! Rejoice! Emmanuel
Shall come to thee, O Israel.

22 December

O come, thou King of nations, show
Thy gentle rule on earth below;
O cornerstone of unity,
Renew us whom thou form'dst from clay.
Rejoice! Rejoice! Emmanuel
Shall come to thee, O Israel.

23 December

O come, O come, Emmanuel
And save thy people Israel,
Our Lord and King, our Law and Light,
Come save us with great power and might.
Rejoice! Rejoice! Emmanuel
Shall come to thee, O Israel.

Tone for the Magnificat:

My soul doth magnify the Lord,
and my spirit hath rejoiced in God my Saviour;
for he hath regarded
the lowliness of his handmaiden.

Rejoice! Rejoice! . . .

For behold from henceforth
all generations shall call me blessed;
for he that is mighty hath magnified me,
and holy is his name.

Rejoice! Rejoice! . . .

And his mercy is on them that fear him,
throughout all generations;
he hath showed strength with his arm,
he hath scattered the proud in the imagination of their hearts.

Rejoice! Rejoice! . . .

He hath put down the mighty from their seat,
and hath exalted the humble and meek;
he hath filled the hungry with good things
and the rich he hath sent empty away.

Rejoice! Rejoice! . . .

He remembering his mercy
hath holpen his servant Israel,
as he promised to our forefathers,
Abraham and his seed for ever.

Rejoice! Rejoice! . . .

Glory be to the Father and to the Son,
and to the Holy Ghost,
as it was in the beginning, is now and ever shall be,
world without end, Amen.

The whole Antiphon is repeated.

An Advent Celebration of Forgiveness and Reconciliation

It would be appropriate to use this service during the first three weeks of Advent.

As the congregation gathers, each person is given an unlit candle.

A suitable hymn or song begins the service. Possible choices might be:

Hark the glad sound! (New English Hymnal 6)
On Jordan's bank the Baptist's cry (New English Hymnal *12*)
Come to set us free (Laudate *81*)
The Advent Prose (New English Hymnal *501*)
or *Come, Saviour, come like dew on the grass* (the version of the same piece in Laudate, no. *95*)

The president may introduce the service with words such as these:

V/. The Lord be with you,
R/. And also with you.

Dear friends in Christ,
with joyful and spiritual expectation
we prepare to celebrate the human birth
of God's all-creating Word.
In order that we may draw more deeply

on the meaning of this wonderful season,
let us listen to the Advent voice:
the voice of the Prophet calling the people
to prepare the way of the Lord;
the voice of John the Baptist
announcing the One who is to come;
the voice of Mary, pledging herself
as the servant of God's purpose.
So in expectation, in penitence, in faith,
let us approach with confidence
the place of God's forgiveness,
that our guilt may be wiped away,
and our hearts opened to receive
the reconciliation which is found in Christ.

Let us pray.

Collect

O God, who through your only Son
fashioned us to be a new creation,
look with kindness on this work of your mercy
and by the coming of Christ
remove from us all trace
of our old and sinful ways.
We make this prayer
through Jesus Christ, the Lord.

or:

God of power,
arise and come to our aid,
and since we are entrapped
and weakened by our sins,
let your wisdom release us
and your strength enable us
to serve you once more in freedom.

We make this prayer
through Jesus Christ our Lord.

The Ministry of the Word

Selections may be made from this list of readings. A suitable responsorial psalm is attached to each of the readings from the Old Testament and the letters of the New Testament.

Old Testament Readings

Genesis 3:1–19
Adam and Eve eat the fruit and are judged by God
Psalm 38:1–4, 21, 22

Isaiah 1:10–20
The Prophet castigates the sinful nation
Psalm 51:11–18

Isaiah 5:1–7
The Parable of the Vineyard
Psalm 80:9–19

Isaiah 55:1–11
Isaiah speaks of the closeness and compassion of God
Psalm 119:145–152

Malachi 3:1–12
I will send my messenger
Psalm 98

Malachi 4:1–5
The day of the Lord
Psalm 1

Texts for Special Services

Readings from the Letters of the New Testament

Romans 5:6–11
Paul writes of the reconciliation brought by Christ
Psalm 32

Romans 12:1–19
Paul names the gifts necessary for the unity of the Church
Psalm 133

2 Corinthians 5:16–21
Paul writes of the new creation in Christ
Psalm 103:1–10

Galatians 5:16–25
Paul names the fruits of the Spirit
Psalm 85

Ephesians 4:1–5, 17–32
Paul writes of the spiritual revolution that is life in Christ
Psalm 95

Ephesians 5:1–14
Paul invites his listeners to live as children of light
Psalm 112

1 John 1:5—2:2
John proclaims the fellowship of Christians with the incarnate Christ
Psalm 100

Acclamation

Revelation 22:17
V/. Alleluia, Alleluia, Alleluia!
R/. Alleluia, Alleluia, Alleluia!
V/. The Spirit and the bride say 'Come!'
Lord Jesus, come in glory!
R/. Alleluia, Alleluia, Alleluia!

Gospel Readings

Matthew 5:1–12
The Beatitudes

Matthew 5:13–20
Jesus fulfils the Law

Matthew 5:21–30
'You have heard it said . . . but I say . . .'

Matthew 5:33–42
The perfect way

Matthew 5:43–48
Love your enemies

Matthew 6:24–34
Seek first the rule of God

Matthew 18:21–35
The king settling accounts with his slaves

Matthew 25:31–46
The sheep and the goats

Luke 15:1–10
Rejoicing in heaven over one repentant sinner

Luke 18:9–14
The Pharisee and the tax collector

Luke 19:1–10
Zacchaeus

John 15:1–11
Live in Christ and bear fruit

A short address may follow the Gospel.

Texts for Special Services

The congregation is invited to stand. The Act of Sorrow follows. The reader should make appropriate pauses in order to allow for reflection.

Presider: Let us ask the Lord to change our hearts,
so that we may desire the blessings of the kingdom.

Reader: Jesus said: 'Blessed are the poor in spirit, for theirs is the kingdom of heaven.'

Save us, Lord,
from our overbearing spirit;
from our self-centredness;
from our addiction to possessions:

All: Come, Lord, and save us!

Reader: Jesus said: 'Blessed are the gentle, for they shall inherit the earth.'

Save us, Lord,
from our anger and bad temper;
from our violence in word and deed;
from our abuse of the earth, our home:

All: Come, Lord, and save us!

Reader: Jesus said: 'Blessed are those who weep, for they shall be comforted.'

Save us, Lord,
from our lack of compassion;
from our indifference to others' grief;
from all that keeps us from true joy:

All: Come, Lord, and save us!

Reader: Jesus said: 'Blessed are those who hunger and thirst after justice, for they shall be satisfied.'

Save us, Lord,
from our lack of justice to those around us;
from the economics which oppress the poor;
from our connivance at the wrong done by others:

All: Come, Lord, and save us!

Reader: Jesus said: 'Blessed are those who show mercy, for they shall receive mercy.'

Save us, Lord,
from our intolerance and judgemental spirit;
from the lack of forgiveness we harbour in our hearts;
from our indifference to one another's need:

All: Come, Lord, and save us!

Reader: Jesus said: 'Blessed are the pure in heart, for they shall see God.'

Save us, Lord,
from all that is crooked in our hearts;
from evil thoughts, lustful feelings and self-indulgence;
from our lack of honesty with ourselves and others:

All: Come, Lord, and save us!

Reader: Jesus said: 'Blessed are those who make peace, for they shall be called children of God.'

Save us, Lord,
from our quarrels and longstanding bitterness;
from our inclination to strife and mischief;
from the abuse and neglect of the young:

All: Come, Lord, and save us!

Reader: Jesus said: 'Blessed are those who suffer persecution for
            the sake of justice, for theirs is the kingdom of heaven.'

            Save us, Lord,
            from intolerance in our hearts and in our world;
            from our neglect of prayer for the oppressed;
            from our silence in the face of injustice:

All: Come, Lord, and save us!

After the Act of Sorrow, a silence is kept.

All then recite together this confession:

Father of all, we come before you
seeking your forgiveness and peace.
We have made burdens for ourselves
and forced others to carry them.
We have done wrong ourselves
and connived at wrongs done by others.
We live so close to suffering
yet are slow to bring relief.
Have pity on us, see the tears
wept for ourselves and for this broken world.
Lay your hands upon us
to heal, forgive and reconcile.
By the gentle working of the Holy Spirit
set us free to be faithful to the gospel
and walk in the way of Jesus.
Amen.

*The members of the congregation then come to the president,
who lays a hand on their head or shoulder and says:*

N. God forgives you. Be at peace.

After receiving the laying on of hands, each person's candle is lit by a server. The people remain standing around the president. When all have received the laying on of hands, the president stretches out hands over them all and says:

Strong and loving God,
through the death and resurrection of your Christ
you have reconciled all things to yourself
and sent the Holy Spirit
for the forgiveness of sins.
Be present to us who await your love;
touch us with your healing hand.
Grant release from our guilt
and pardon for our offences.
Set us free from the burdens
that oppress our spirit.
Reconcile us to you in peace
and to those about us in mutual charity.
We ask this through Christ our Lord.

or:

God of compassion,
accept the prayer of those
who bow their heads before you
in sorrow for their sins.
Grant them forgiveness
and set them free to walk with joy
in the way of your commandments.
We ask this in the name of Jesus,
our Saviour, now and for ever.

The president gives the absolution:

In the name of Christ
who forgives and heals and raises up,
and by the ministry of the Holy Spirit in the Church,
you are absolved from all your sins.

And may the blessing of almighty God,
the Father, the Son and the Holy Spirit,
be with you and remain with you always.

All exchange a sign of peace.

A suitable hymn of thanksgiving may conclude the service.

PART SEVEN

TEXTS FOR SPECIAL
SERVICES OF CHRISTMAS

Like Advent, Christmas has given rise to many customs connected with the Church's worship. Particularly for children, these customs offer an opportunity for colourful insights into the meaning and celebration of Christmas. Outlines and prayers are given here for a blessing of the Christmas Crib, a service for Christmas Eve and a blessing of gifts for the festival of the Epiphany. Where children are present, they should play a prominent part in the services.

A Blessing of the Christmas Crib

Some churches have the crib blessing associated with the Midnight Eucharist, others at a service for children on Christmas Eve. The form given here may be adapted for use on either occasion.

The crib is empty of all figures. Each figure should be carried in procession to the crib and placed appropriately. A suitable song may be sung. When all the figures are in place, the president or other minister may say:

Christ, the firstborn of creation
is born among us as a little child.
We make the crib to mark that moment
when the humanity of God was revealed.

Let us pray.

After a pause, the minister says one of the following prayers:

Father,
bless this crib
and keep before our eyes this Christmas
the image of your eternal Son,
who is one with you and the Holy Spirit,
now and for ever.

or:

Father of all goodness,
let this crib recall
that Jesus is one with you as God,
and yet came to be one with us
as the child laid in the manger.
Let his mind be in us,
and let our hearts be lifted up
to contemplate the glory
that is your divine humanity.
We ask this through Christ our Lord.

An Evening Service for Christmas Eve

Outlines for a more formal Vigil Service or Evening Prayer are given on pp. 47ff.

However, a simpler service may be appropriate, particularly where it might be celebrated with children. The outline that follows is for a service at the Crib. A good time for the service is in mid afternoon, just as it is beginning to get dark.

The Advent wreath will be used for the last time. The candles will be decorated with symbols indicating the prophet Isaiah, King David, John the Baptist and the Blessed Virgin Mary. The centre candle will carry symbols of Christ (see above. p. 102).

The congregation and ministers or leaders gather around the

Crib, which should be empty of figures and unlit. An appropriate opening song or hymn may be sung.

The minister begins the service:

Minister: From the One who is and who was and who is to
come, grace, mercy and peace be with you all.

All: And also with you.

The Minister welcomes the congregation and introduces the service, in these or similar words:

Today, this Christmas Eve as darkness falls,
we remember the holy birth that brought us light.
We rejoice that God has come to us.
We are struck with wonder at this newborn baby
reaching out hands toward his Mother;
for these are the hands that set the stars in their places
and formed us out of clay to be his likeness.
The One who made this human body
now comes to share its mortality,
to save it from the nothingness of death
and glorify it as his own for ever.

We light the candles on the Advent wreath,
to remember those who saw Christ coming
and were filled with the same joyful expectation
that now fills our hearts.

The first candle is lit. A reader says:

For Isaiah, prophet of God, who said:
'The people who walked in darkness
have seen a great light.'

All: Glory to God in the highest
and peace to his people on earth.

The second candle is lit. A reader says:

For David the King, the ancestor of Christ,
the singer of God's praises, who proclaimed:
'The Lord is my light and my salvation.'

All: Glory to God in the highest
and peace to his people on earth.

The third candle is lit. A reader says:

For John the Baptist, herald of the Light,
who spoke of the one who was to come and said:
'He will baptize you with the Holy Spirit and with fire.'

All: Glory to God in the highest
and peace to his people on earth.

The fourth candle is lit. A reader says:

For Mary, Mother of God,
who carried within her womb
the light of all the nations.

All: Glory to God in the highest
and peace to his people on earth.

The candle representing Christ is lit. A reader says:

Jesus Christ, the Light of the world:
no darkness can quench this light;
no night shall cover it.

All: Glory to God in the highest
and peace to his people on earth.

A carol or hymn is sung.

The account of the birth of Jesus is read from Saint Luke's Gospel (Luke 2:1–20). If desired, it might be read in the form of a dialogue between two readers like this:

Reader 1:   Tell us, whose birth is this?
Whose is the story?
Who has appeared on earth?

Reader 2:   Jesus Christ, his birth,
Jesus Christ, his story:
God has appeared on earth!

Reader 1:   Tell us, when was this birth?
What day? What season of the year?

Reader 2:   The days of Caesar Augustus,
the census of the entire world;
while Quirinius was governor of Syria.
Will you hear the story of Christ's birth?
Will you listen for his coming?

Reader 1:   Yes, we will listen.
Tell us what you have heard and seen.

Reader 2:   A man called Joseph
went up from Galilee to Judaea,
to Bethlehem, his own town,
the city of David, his ancestor.
He went to be registered in the census.
With him went Mary, to whom he was engaged
and who was expecting a child.
While they were there, her time arrived,
the time for Mary to give birth.
She brought her firstborn son into the world
and wrapped him in strips of cloth
and laid him in a manger,
since there was no room for them at the inn.

Reader 1:   Shepherds there were, out in the fields,
keeping their sheep safe in the night.
Then suddenly the Messenger of God stood before
   them,
the glory of God was shining all around them
and they were so afraid.
But the Messenger said: 'Do not be afraid.
I bring word to you, good news,
joy for you and for the whole people.
For you a child is born today in David's town;
this child is the Saviour,
this child is Christ the Lord.
Here is the sign you must look for:
you will find a baby,
wrapped in strips of cloth,
lying in a manger.

Reader 2:   In that instant, huge numbers of heavenly beings
stood with the Messenger and shouted out:

All: Glory to God in the highest
and peace to his people on earth!

Reader 1:   The messengers had gone. The shepherds said:
'Let's go then, go to Bethlehem and see
what has happened, what God has shown us.'
They came quickly and found Mary and Joseph
and the baby lying in the manger.
When they saw it all, they told their story,
what they had been told about this child.
All who heard it were amazed at what the
   shepherds said.
Mary, however, treasured all their words
and kept them fresh in her heart.
So the shepherds went back,
singing the praise and glory of God
for all they had heard and seen.
It was exactly as they had been told.

A suitable song may be sung.

The minister may give a short talk on the meaning of Christmas.

The Crib is now prepared. See p. 127 for the Blessing of the Crib.

When the Crib has been prepared, the Christ-candle from the Advent wreath is placed on a candlestick in front of the Crib.

Carols may be sung around the Crib.

The service should conclude with prayers such as these:

Minister:
Let us pray to Christ,
the eternal Word made flesh,
manifest in human birth.

All: Christ Jesus, hear our prayer.

At your birth,
heaven cried out glory and peace:
shed your peace throughout the world.

All: Christ Jesus, hear our prayer.

Sun of righteousness,
you revealed your glory in our human body:
pour upon us your holy light.

All: Christ Jesus, hear our prayer.

Image of God,
make us obedient to your teaching,
that we may honour you by faith and love.

All: Christ Jesus, hear our prayer.

God-with-us,
you make the whole creation new:
create in us a new heart and new spirit.

All: Christ Jesus, hear our prayer.

Eternal King,
remember us when you come in your kingdom
and teach us to pray:

All: Our Father . . .

The minister may end the service with one of the collects for Christmas Eve on p. 24.

A Blessing of Gifts for Epiphany

At the preparation of the Lord's Table in the Eucharist (or an appropriate point at the main service) of Epiphany, the gifts of the Magi may be presented as follows:

The procession with the gifts makes its way to the altar. At the Eucharist, the bread and wine should be brought up last in the procession.

This hymn may be sung (to the melody 'Quem pastores laudavere', New English Hymnal *387):*

Christ has come! His star is risen
Brighter than the lights of heaven;
Christ the long-desired of nations,
Christ the light of nations all.

Wise men to the child come bearing
Gifts, his destiny declaring;
Gold, incense and myrrh they give him,
Christ the light of nations all.

Gold a royal rank discloses,
Incense to a god arises,
Myrrh anoints the dead for burial,
Christ the light of nations all.

King of peace who comes to rule us!
God who ever dwells among us!
Christ who died and rose victorious!
Christ the light of nations all.

*A member of the congregation brings ornaments signifying gold.
The following is said as the president or deacon receives the gold:*

Gold for a King!
May Christ, the King,
bestow upon the world
the gifts of unity and peace,
for his kingdom abides,
now and for ever.

*A member of the congregation brings incense grains. The follow-
ing is said:*

Incense for the holy One!
May Christ, the Creator Word,
renew the holiness of creation
and fill the heavens and the earth
with the majesty of God's glory,
now and for ever.

*A member of the congregation brings a box of myrrh. The
following is said:*

Myrrh for One who is to die!
May the risen power of Christ
gather all peoples together,
so that from the rising to the setting sun

a pure offering may be made to God,
now and for ever.

In the Eucharist, the bread and wine are brought up and presented after the gold, incense and myrrh. The bread and cup are prepared. The president takes the bread and cup. The president may place the incense that has been offered in the thurible and incense the table and gifts. The people may then be incensed.

If gold, incense and myrrh have been brought, then the prayer over the gifts on p. 40 is not used. In its place, the president recites this Epiphany prayer over the gifts:

In your kindness, Lord,
look upon the gifts of your Church.
In gold, incense and myrrh
we celebrate Christ
as King and God,
in whose dying is our life.
Through this bread and cup
unite us with him in his self-offering,
and in his resurrection, now and for ever.

PART EIGHT

TEXTS FOR FEASTS AND SAINTS' DAYS DURING ADVENT–EPIPHANY

The following festivals occur during the Season of Advent/ Christmas/Epiphany.

30 November Saint Andrew, Apostle

Andrew is recorded as being the brother of Simon Peter and, like him, a native of Bethsaida in Galilee. One of the first disciples to be called by Christ, he brought Peter to Jesus. He is remembered as one of the Twelve and is honoured as the Patron Saint of several nations including Scotland, Russia and Greece. In the Anglican tradition, Saint Andrew's Tide is a season of prayer for the missionary Church.

Scripture-related opening prayer

God, our salvation,
you called Saint Andrew the fisherman
to cast the nets of your gospel
among the nations of the earth.
Give your Church boldness in its preaching
and a receptive heart to all who listen,
so that you may be glorified
by all who become your disciples.
We make this prayer through Jesus Christ our Lord.

Opening prayer

God of all who believe,
you set the Christian faith firm
on the foundations laid by your Apostles.
Open our hearts once more to their teaching
as we celebrate the calling of Saint Andrew
and his birthday into eternal life.
We make this prayer through Jesus Christ our Lord.

Acclamation

Matthew 4:19
V/. Alleluia, Alleluia, Alleluia.
R/. Alleluia, Alleluia, Alleluia.
V/. 'Follow me,' said the Lord,
'and I will make you fish for people.'
R/. Alleluia, Alleluia, Alleluia.

Intercession

Lord God,
let the example of Saint Andrew
strengthen and inspire your Church
to make your name known
to every nation on earth.
We ask this through Christ our Lord.

Prayer over the Gifts

God of our joy,
let the praise we bring to your table
in honour of Saint Andrew the Apostle
strengthen us in our service of your Gospel.
We ask this through Jesus Christ our Lord.

Eucharistic Preface

It is truly right and just, our duty and our salvation,
always and everywhere to give you thanks,
Lord, holy Father, almighty and eternal God.

In these holy mysteries of salvation
we celebrate Saint Andrew
who, by his preaching of Christ your Son
and by the example of his martyrdom,
showed himself a true brother to Simon Peter
and shared in the glory of those
called by Christ to be his Apostles.

And so we join with angels and saints
in this, their joyful shout of praise: Holy . . .

Prayer after Communion

God of the living,
let this sacrament
bring us to that eternal life
which awaited Saint Andrew
for his faithful witness to Christ.
We ask this through Jesus Christ our Lord.

8 December The Conception of the Virgin Mary

*This feast originated in the Eastern parts of the Church as 'The
Conception of Mary by Saint Anne'. It spread to the Western
churches where it underwent a transformation. In the medieval
period and later, it became a focus of a doctrinal development
about the atonement which, as part of an understanding of sin
and grace, came to view the Virgin Mary as having been conceived (the 'Immaculate Conception') without original sin, by a
singular grace of Christ the Redeemer.*

However, the older sense of this festival is simply a celebration of God's gift of a child to Joachim and Anne and the divine choice of Mary to be the mother of the Incarnate Word.

In Common Worship *the Conception is kept simply as a festival of Mary, without any particular theological focus.*

Scripture-related opening prayer

God of all grace,
you chose the Virgin Mary
from the moment of her conception
and prepared her to give our flesh and blood
to your Incarnate Word.
Grant that as you blessed her
with obedience to carry out your plan,
so you will complete in us
the gracious work you have begun.
We ask this through Jesus Christ,
who is one with you and the Holy Spirit,
now and for ever.

Opening prayer

God, our life,
you began the work of redemption
when Mary, the Daughter of Zion,
was conceived in her mother's womb.
You made her heart receptive to your call;
make us likewise hear your word and keep it.
We ask this through Jesus Christ our Lord.

Acclamation

Luke 1:49
V/. The Almighty has worked wonders for me
and holy is his name.

Intercession

God of wisdom,
who chose the Virgin Mary
to take her part in your plan of salvation,
let your Church learn from her
a strong and joyful acceptance of your call
that, like her, we may place our hope
in your promise alone.
We ask this through Christ our Lord.

Prayer over the Gifts

At your table, Lord,
we lift our hearts in praise
and honour the Mother of Christ.
Let your blessings make us
a living sacrifice to your glory.
We ask this through Christ our Lord.

Eucharistic Preface

It is truly right and just, our duty and our salvation,
always and everywhere to give you thanks,
Lord, holy Father, almighty and eternal God.

You chose the Virgin Mary
to bear your eternal Son,
and by his redeeming power
you prepared in her womb a holy place
for the great mystery of the Incarnation.

And so, with angels and saints,
we exult and glorify your holy name: Holy . . .

Prayer after Communion

Let the holy feast which we have shared, O God,
make us open to you,
just as Mary placed herself at the disposal of the One
who was to be born of her,
Christ Jesus, our Saviour, now and for ever.

26 December Saint Stephen, Deacon, Protomartyr

*The day after the celebration of Christ's earthly birth, the
Church commemorates the heavenly birth of Saint Stephen.
Stephen, a Greek-speaking Jew, was one of the seven men
appointed by the Apostles for service to the Church (Acts 6:1–6).
He was stoned to death after preaching with wisdom and the
Spirit (Acts 6:8–10). He called for the forgiveness of those who
were killing him. This feast has been celebrated in the Church
from the fourth century.*

Scripture-related opening prayer

Faithful God,
who revealed your glory
to the holy martyr Stephen
and showed him the Son of Man
standing at your right hand,
keep us steadfast in our witness to your truth
and faithful in the service of our neighbour
that we may know the eternal blessings
promised to all who are faithful to your word.
We make this prayer through Jesus Christ,
who is one with you and the Holy Spirit,
now and for ever.

Opening prayer

Grant, Lord,
that as we celebrate
the birthday into eternal life
of your Martyr Stephen,
so we may learn
from the boldness of his teaching
and the constancy of his witness unto death.
We make this prayer through Christ our Lord.

Acclamation

Psalm 118:26
V/. Blessed is the One who comes
in the name of the Lord.

Intercession

God of truth,
guide us by your light
and show us your glory,
that your people may rejoice
to be called Christians
and truly become what you call us to be.
We ask this through Christ our Lord.

Prayer over the Gifts

God of the just,
on this feast of Saint Stephen
open our lips to proclaim your praise,
and make us your eloquent witnesses
through service of our neighbour.
We ask this through Christ our Lord.

Eucharistic Preface

It is truly right and just, our duty and our salvation,
always and everywhere to give you thanks,
Lord, holy Father, almighty and eternal God.

You called Stephen the Deacon
to proclaim the gospel
and shed his blood for the name of Jesus.
Stephen took up the words of his Master
and spoke what Christ had spoken on the cross,
and as he entrusted himself to the risen Lord
he prayed for the forgiveness of his enemies.

And so, with angels and all saints,
we glorify your holy name: Holy . . .

Prayer after Communion

God of mercy,
in the birth of Christ
you bring salvation to the world.
Grant that this celebration of your Martyr Stephen
may bring joy to your people.
We ask this through Christ our Lord.

27 December Saint John, Apostle and Evangelist

*Both John and his brother James left their nets at the call of Jesus
and became disciples. John was 'the disciple whom Jesus loved'
and the author of the Fourth Gospel, the three letters and (with
less certainty) the Book of Revelation.*

Scripture-related opening prayer

God of steadfast love,
you called John, the evangelist,
to declare what he had heard and seen

and to proclaim the Word made Flesh.
Grant that we, receiving the teaching
of the Beloved Disciple,
may have fellowship with you
and communion with one another.
We make this prayer through Jesus Christ,
who is one with you and the Holy Spirit,
now and for ever.

Opening prayer

All-powerful God,
through the blessed Apostle John
you unfolded for us
the mystery of your eternal Word.
Let this divine Wisdom fill our hearts
and illuminate our minds
that we may put our faith in Christ
and find life through his name.

Acclamation

John 1:14
V/. The Word was made flesh
and dwelt among us.

Intercession

Lord, look kindly on your Church,
that, guided by the teaching of the Apostle John,
your people may understand more deeply
the Christ whom he proclaimed.
We ask this through Christ our Lord.

Prayer over the Gifts

God of all grace,
as we come to your table

open our lips in praise
and so direct our lives
that we may worship you
in spirit and in truth.
We ask this through Christ our Lord.

Eucharistic Preface

We lift our hearts to you,
God eternal, true and faithful;
to you we offer thanks and praise
as we celebrate the memory of Saint John.

The Lord bestowed on John
a lasting place and privilege among his own.
As he hung upon the cross
Christ willed that his beloved disciple
should be a son to his own Mother.
The love with which Jesus loved him
transformed him from fisherman to apostle
and gave him a more than mortal insight
to perceive and proclaim
the uncreated Godhead of Christ the Word.

And so, with angels and saints,
we glorify your holy name: Holy . . .

Prayer after Communion

God, our provider,
you make us partakers of Christ,
the living bread and true vine.
Through this most holy gift
may we abide always in him
and bear the fruit
which you prepare for his disciples.
We ask this through Christ our Lord.

28 December The Holy Innocents, Martyrs

The Gospel of Saint Matthew records how Herod massacred the infants of the Bethlehem district in an attempt to kill the child Jesus. The Holy Innocents have been honoured as Martyrs on this day from the sixth century. This feast is also an opportunity to remember the suffering and death of all innocent people, particularly children.

Scripture-related opening prayer

God,
consoler of the comfortless,
you glorified the children
who were martyrs of Christ
even before they could speak his name.
Amidst the violence of this present age
confirm our hope in your kingdom
where innocence is vindicated,
the exile finds a home
and those who are steadfast receive eternal life.
We make this prayer through Jesus Christ,
who is one with you and the Holy Spirit,
now and for ever.

Opening prayer

God, whose glory
the Holy Innocents proclaimed
not by their words but by their death;
give to all your people
the strength to testify to our faith
both by our words and through our lives.
We make this prayer through Jesus Christ our Lord.

Acclamation

Psalm 124:7
V/. Our help is in the name of the Lord,
who has made heaven and earth.

Intercession

Let your Church rejoice, Lord,
to celebrate the martyrdom of the Innocents,
for you choose the weak and make them strong
in bearing witness to you,
through Jesus Christ our Lord.

Prayer over the Gifts

At your table, O God,
let all be remembered
who suffer for your name,
even as they are numbered
among those you have redeemed
through Christ our Lord.

Eucharistic Preface

It is truly right and just, our duty and our salvation,
always and everywhere to give you thanks,
Lord, holy Father, almighty and eternal God.

We acknowledge your grace in the Holy Innocents:
your power is revealed where strength is least
and martyrdom precedes the power of speech.
For Christ they suffered,
even though they did not know him,
and you have not let them lose their reward;
but rather, in the shedding of their blood
you have enacted the saving birth of baptism
and bestowed on them the martyrs' crown.

And so, with angels and saints,
we exult and glorify your holy name: Holy . . .

Prayer after Communion

Lord,
at the birth of your Son
you bestowed on the Holy Innocents
a new and heavenly birth
as martyrs for the name of Jesus.
Grant to us, who receive this holy sacrament,
the fullness of salvation
in fellowship with them.
We ask this through Christ our Lord.

1 January The Naming and Circumcision of Jesus

*The Festival of the Naming and Circumcision of Jesus represents
the fullness of the Covenant, both the Old Covenant symbolized
by circumcision and the New sealed by the Holy Spirit.
Circumcision was the outward sign of the Covenant made with
Abraham, into which Jesus was initiated in order to found a
covenant with all men and women, who by the Holy Spirit are
called into an adoptive relationship with the Father. The feast
also celebrates the name of Jesus, the only name by which we
may be saved (cf. Acts 4:12).*

Scripture-related opening prayer

God, Father of all,
in the fullness of time
you sent your Son to be born of a woman
as a subject of your holy Law.
Fill us with wonder
at this great blessing you have bestowed,
that we who are your children in Christ

may be faithful to the Spirit of adoption
which you have sent into our hearts.
We make this prayer through Jesus Christ,
who is one with you and the Holy Spirit,
now and for ever.

Opening prayer

God, rich in mercy,
you have called us to a heavenly destiny
in your beloved Son.
Grant that as he shares with us
the human nature of this creation
so we may become your new creation
as sharers in his divine life
by the power of the Holy Spirit.
We make this prayer through Jesus Christ our Lord.

Acclamation

Philippians 2:10, 11
V/. Let every knee bend at the name of Jesus
and every tongue confess that Jesus is Lord.

Intercession

God of all grace,
make the hearts of your people receptive
to the wonders of your love,
that we may always ponder with awe
the things that we celebrate with joy.
We ask this through Christ our Lord.

Prayer over the Gifts

God, the beginning and fulfilment
of all that is good and true,

let our delight in your gifts of grace
bring forth from our hearts
a song of thanks and praise.
We ask this through Christ our Lord.

Eucharistic Preface

It is truly right and just, our duty and our salvation,
always and everywhere to give you thanks,
Lord, holy Father, almighty and eternal God,
through Jesus Christ our Lord.

To redeem us from the burden of the Law,
Christ accepted circumcision as that Law required.
In this, he affirmed the ordinance of old
and fashioned our human nature anew.
From his fullness we receive your grace,
and in his name we gain our freedom,
since by his Incarnation
he enfolds and enriches
the poverty of our human nature.

Through him, therefore, with all the powers of heaven,
we glorify your holy Name: Holy . . .

Prayer after Communion

God of salvation,
in this holy feast you call us
into communion with Christ.
Let us, who bear his name,
extend that communion to all
whom you are calling to be your children.
We ask this through Christ our Lord.

PART NINE

OTHER MATERIAL FOR THE MAIN SERVICE OF SUNDAY

The Kyrie Eleison

The acclamation Kyrie eleison *is common to nearly all Christian liturgies. It is translated into English as 'Lord, have mercy', though such a version sounds more penitential than is probably intended by the original Greek, whose overtones of gentleness and compassion do not quite fit with the more forensic idea of 'mercy'.*

The Kyrie *was most often used as a response for a litany. However, in* The Book of Common Prayer, *it was adapted to form a response to the Ten Commandments at the beginning of the Communion Service. In* Common Worship *it is used at the beginning of the Eucharist.*

In its ancient Greek form, Kyrie eleison *was intended as an address to Christ, the 'Lord' or Kyrios of Saint Paul's letters. In its later (Western) usage as a ninefold acclamation it came to be addressed to the Father, the Son and the Spirit in turn. This may have been due to the Latin adaptation* Christe eleison – *intended perhaps originally to make the christic address of the whole acclamation clear, but in fact having the longer-term effect of making the acclamation Trinitarian. In the later Middle Ages the* Kyrie *was 'troped' or interspersed with texts reflecting this newer understanding, relating to the roles of Father, Son and Spirit.*

The following words for use with the acclamation Kyrie eleison *have been prepared with the older, Christological, meaning in mind.*

Advent

You came to gather all peoples
into the kingdom of God's peace:

You come in word and sacrament
to call us again to holiness:

You will come again in glory
to judge and save your people:

Christ, defender of the poor:

Jesus, refuge of the lowly:

Christ, rock of our salvation:

You came to visit your people in peace:

You came to seek out and save the lost:

You came to begin a world made new:

Wisdom of the Most High
filling the whole creation:

Lord of your people,
giver of the law of love:

Root of Jesse, sign to the peoples,
desire of all nations:

Key of David, you open and none will close,
you free those held fast by death:

Dayspring, you are the radiant eternal light,
and sun of righteousness:

King of nations, for you the whole earth waits,
Emmanuel, God-with-us:

Christmas

Son of God, who at your human birth
became our brother:

Son of Man, who through your human nature
have experienced our weakness:

Only-Begotten, who in your risen flesh
have bound us into one body:

King of peace:

Light in darkness:

Image of humanity renewed:

Mighty God, Prince of peace:

Son of God, Son of Mary:

Word made Flesh, glory of the Father:

Christ,
in whom heaven and earth are one:

Jesus,
in whom mercy and faithfulness have met:

Christ,
in whom righteousness and peace have embraced:

Epiphany and Baptism of Christ

Christ, eternal King:

Jesus, eternal priest:

Christ, sacrifice of peace:

Before you, Lord Jesus,
all kings shall fall down in worship:

In your presence, Lord Jesus,
all nations shall serve God's glory:

In your abiding life, Lord Jesus,
we have our access to the Father:

Christ, by your baptism
the waters were hallowed to save us:

Christ, at your baptism
the gift of the Holy Spirit was revealed:

Christ, at your baptism
the Father acclaimed you as his Son:

Christ, manifested in the flesh,
vindicated in the Spirit:

Christ, seen by angels,
proclaimed among the nations:

Christ, believed in by the world,
taken up in glory:

A Penitential Act

*This short Penitential Act might be used at the beginning of a
service in Advent.*

After the processional hymn or Introit (and the words In the
name of the Father . . .*), the president greets the people:*

President:
From the One who is and who was and who is to come,
grace, mercy and peace be with you all.

R/. And also with you.

The president may briefly introduce the act of repentance.

Another minister says:

V/. Lord, have mercy on your people:
R/. For we have sinned against you.
V/. Lord, show us your mercy:
R/. And grant us your salvation.
V/. Lord, let your love be upon us:
R/. For we place all our trust in you.

The president gives the absolution:

May Christ who came among us
forgive our sins.
May Christ who is with us always
heal what is broken in us.
May Christ who is to come in glory
do justice for us and save us,
now and for ever:

R/. Amen.

Enthronement of the Gospels or Scriptures

From the time of the first ecumenical councils, it has been customary on occasion to bring the Book of Gospels into the worship space in procession and display or 'enthrone' it. The bishops of the Roman Catholic Church, gathered for the Second Vatican Council in 1963, enthroned the Gospels at the beginning of their deliberations, so as to put themselves in obedience to the word of Christ.

On the Sundays of Advent and Christmas, particularly if the Main Service is not the Eucharist, the ceremony of 'enthroning the scriptures', that is, bringing the Bible, Lectionary or Book of the Gospels into the congregation, might be appropriate.

The Entrance with the Holy Scriptures

Depending on which books are used, readers or other ministers may take part in the entrance procession carrying the books. The bearers may be accompanied by members of the congregation carrying lighted candles.

It might be appropriate to have a separate procession for the Scriptures, which might take a long route through the congregation to allow as many people as possible to come close to the Scriptures.

If a separate Book of the Gospels is used, it should come last in processional order.

Here are some of the many hymns that might be used:

O heavenly Word of God on high (New English Hymnal 2)
God has spoken (Hymns for Today's Church 248)
Thanks be to God whose word was spoken (Hymns for Today's Church 255)
Praise to you, O Christ our Saviour (Laudate 200)

The book(s) are placed in suitable locations in the worship area, perhaps upon lecterns or stands. Candles might be lit and placed beside them.

The following responses might be used to end the rite:

V/. Blessed are you, God of all creation:
R/. The Word by whom the universe was formed.

V/. Blessed are you, God of our salvation:
R/. The Word made flesh in Jesus, child of Mary.

V/. Blessed are you, God of holiness:
R/. The Holy Spirit, who speaks in the Scriptures.

or:

V/. In the beginning was the word:
R/. And the word was with God, and the word was God.
V/. By him all things came to be:
R/. In him was life, the light of mortals.
V/. The word was made flesh:
R/. And pitched a tent among us.
V/. We beheld his glory:
R/. The Father's only Son,
full of grace and truth.

The following prayer may be used:

Holy Spirit of God,
rest upon this assembly
in its hearing of the Scriptures,
in its reflection upon their words
and in its discipleship of Christ,
that every knee may bow before his name,
who lives and reigns for ever and ever.

*The Prayer Book Collect for the Second Sunday of Advent
would also be appropriate in this ceremony.*

For the *Agnus Dei*

The Agnus Dei *is a litany, with* Have mercy on us *as its response.*
Common Worship *gives two forms, with either of which the
texts given here are compatible.*

Lamb of God *was introduced into the Roman Mass from the
East, probably in the eighth century* AD. *It was a chant sung to
cover the breaking of the eucharistic bread and pouring of the
cups, a procedure that would originally have taken some time, as
small leavened loaves were used and the wine had to be poured*

from one chalice into several smaller ones and mixed with wine that had not been 'consecrated'. To allow for this, the chant was simply extended, with as many repetitions of Lamb of God . . . *as required.*

Other ancient Latin rites such as the Ambrosian of Milan did not use the Agnus Dei. *To cover the breaking and preparation of the Communion, a responsorial chant known as the* Confractorium *(i.e. 'for the breaking') was sung, which varied with the season or feast. As an alternative, some suggestions are made here for similar responsorial texts that refer directly to the action.*

Modern practice with the Agnus Dei, *where an extended setting is required, has been to 'trope' the text and vary the invocations. Some examples are given below. If they are to be sung, a simple setting of the petition* Have mercy on us *may be sung, and the invocation spoken or sung to a simple chant formula.*

V/. Lamb of God, you are our Passover and our peace:
R/. *Have mercy on us.*
V/. Lamb of God, you are our Sacrifice of reconciliation:
R/. *Have mercy on us.*
V/. Lamb of God, you are our great High Priest:
R/. *Have mercy on us.*

Lamb of God, true and living bread:
Lamb of God, true and life-giving vine:
Lamb of God, food for our earthly pilgrimage:

Lamb of God, Shepherd of the flock:
Lamb of God, Shepherd who lays down his life:
Lamb of God, Risen Shepherd of souls:

Lamb of God, image and likeness of the Father:
Lamb of God, humbling yourself and accepting death:
Lamb of God, name above all names:

Anthems for the Breaking of the Bread

Christ our Passover is sacrificed for us:
Therefore let us keep the feast.
He is our peace, who has reconciled us to God:
Therefore let us keep the feast.
The marriage of the Lamb has come:
Therefore let us keep the feast.

The bread which we break
is a sharing in the body of Christ:
We being many are one body,
for we all share in the one bread.
Into one body we were all baptized,
and one Spirit was given us all to drink:
We being many are one body,
for we all share in the one bread.

My flesh is food indeed,
and my blood is drink indeed, says the Lord.
My flesh is food indeed,
and my blood is drink indeed, says the Lord.
Those who eat my flesh and drink my blood
dwell in me and I in them.
My flesh is food indeed,
and my blood is drink indeed, says the Lord.

Whoever eats this bread will live for ever:
Whoever eats this bread will live for ever.
The true bread comes down from heaven:
Whoever eats this bread will live for ever.
Whoever believes in me shall not hunger:
Whoever eats this bread will live for ever.

The disciples knew the Lord
in the breaking of the bread.
The disciples knew the Lord
in the breaking of the bread.

The bread that we break
is the communion of the body of Christ.
The disciples knew the Lord
in the breaking of the bread.
Though we are many, we are one body,
for we all share in the one bread.
The disciples knew the Lord
in the breaking of the bread.

Wisdom has prepared her table,
she has mixed her wine.
Blessed are those who are called
to the supper of the Lamb.
Come, eat of my bread,
and drink the wine I have prepared.
Blessed are those who are called
to the supper of the Lamb.
Listen to me and eat what is good,
delight yourselves in my rich food.
Blessed are those who are called
to the supper of the Lamb.

You shall eat and drink at my table in my kingdom,
says the Lord.
You shall eat and drink at my table in my kingdom,
says the Lord.
The Spirit and the Bride say 'Come.'
You shall eat and drink at my table in my kingdom,
says the Lord.
Let everyone who hears, say 'Come.'
You shall eat and drink at my table in my kingdom,
says the Lord.
Let everyone who is thirsty, come.
You shall eat and drink at my table in my kingdom,
says the Lord.

PART TEN

A EUCHARISTIC PRAYER

This prayer is based on the Eucharistic Prayer printed in Volume II of this series. Though its experimental nature may limit its use in churches that have an officially fixed eucharistic prayer tradition, the text attempts to show how in principle the prayer may be made responsive to the seasons of the Christian Year in ways other than the use of the variable preface. The link between the acclamation *Holy, Holy, Holy Lord* and the narrative of the Lord's Supper seems to offer possibilities for seasonal variation of a more generic kind than is found in the prefaces. It is such possibilities that are explored here.

Seasonal variation in the body of the Eucharistic Canon over and beyond the opening thanksgiving has a long history in the churches of the West. In the ancient liturgies of Gaul and the Iberian peninsula, there was more or less a different Eucharistic Prayer for each Sunday and festival. In the Roman Church, the so-called 'Canon' (the Roman form of the Eucharistic Prayer after the *Sanctus*) had variable passages within it for the five great feasts of the year and for certain occasions such as baptism, ordination and marriage.

In the text printed below, one of the Advent or Christmas prefaces in the body of the text will be used to form the first part of this prayer up to the recitation or singing of the *Holy, Holy*, acclamation.

This prayer contains acclamations for the congregation. The idea of having acclamations in the Eucharistic Prayer after the *Sanctus* has in recent years become a feature of prayers in many churches. There is nothing new in this. Acclamations are common in the anaphoras of the Eastern churches and also in the non-Roman Latin eucharistic prayers of Gaul and Spain. Where these acclamations are used, the question is often raised as to their appropriateness. Sometimes critics have suggested that they are merely ornamental and not essential to the flow of the prayer.

The acclamations contained in the body of this Eucharistic Prayer are in fact integral to the sense and dynamic of the Eucharist. In the opening section and again in the section beginning 'God most high, look upon this Eucharist . . .', it is the people together with the speaker who make the *epiklesis* – the plea that the Holy Spirit come and fulfil the role announced in the preceding words. Again, during the narrative of the Last Supper, the people make the 'Amen' that, as is the case at the reception of Communion, expresses their desire to become engaged in the movement of Christ's self-offering.

After the Acclamation Holy, Holy, Holy Lord *the speaker continues:*

(Advent)
Father, you are the Holy One,
source of all being, worthy of all praise.
Blessed is Jesus, your Christ,
whose coming we acclaim
and whose return we await.
For Christ will glorify this mortal body
through the gift of his flesh,
the sacrifice offered once and for all time
in the power of the Holy Spirit.

(Christmas)
Father, you are the Holy One,
source of all being, worthy of all praise.
Blessed is Jesus the Christ,
your Word incarnate among us.
From his fullness we now receive
the gift of his body and blood,
the sacrifice offered once and for all time
in the power of the Holy Spirit.

(Epiphany)
Father, you are the Holy One,
source of all being, worthy of all praise.
Blessed is Jesus, your Christ,
revealed in our human body
to make us partakers in his glorious body
through his flesh and blood,
the sacrifice offered once and for all time
in the power of the Holy Spirit.

R/. **Amen. Come, Holy Spirit.**

When the hour had come
for Christ freely to give himself up,
he took bread and said the blessing,
broke the bread and gave it to his disciples, saying:
'Take, eat; this is my body which is given for you.
Do this for the remembrance of me.'

R/. **Amen.**

In the same way, after supper,
he took the cup of wine and gave you thanks,
gave the cup to his disciples and said:
'Drink this, all of you;
this is my blood of the new covenant,
which is shed for you and for many
for the forgiveness of sins.
Do this, as often as you drink it,
for the remembrance of me.'

R/. **Amen.**

Father, mindful of this command,
we hold in remembrance
the saving work of Christ:
the death that has destroyed our death,

the rising that promises the glory of all flesh,
the return that will bring your justice
to the living and the dead.
Thus in thanksgiving we bring before you
the one, holy and living sacrifice.

V/. Great is the mystery of faith:
R/. **Christ has died . . .**

God most high, look upon this Eucharist
sanctified by the Holy Spirit,
and sanctify us who receive these gifts;
unite us in the one living bread
as partakers in the body of Christ,
and through the one cup of his blood
let us taste communion in the Holy Spirit
and the joy of the age to come.

R/. **Amen. Come, Holy Spirit.**

Gracious God, renew the life of your Church:
remember N. our Bishop and all ministers
who break and share the living bread among us.

R/. **Lord, remember.**

Remember those broken in body or spirit:
give them peace in the glorious wounds
by which we have been healed.

R/. **Lord, remember.**

Remember us all, both living and departed,
in communion with (Saint N. and all) your saints;
gather your Church together in Christ,
in whom all things in heaven and on earth

are blessed, and made holy,
and raised up before your face eternally.

Through Christ, and with Christ, and in Christ:

R/. **Amen**

in the unity of the Holy Spirit:

R/. **Amen**

all honour and glory is yours,
almighty God and Father,
both now and for ever:

R/. **Amen.**

SOURCES AND ACKNOWLEDGEMENTS

The texts contained in this book come from several sources.

The process of creating texts for worship is complex and any writer will unconsciously find that they have used sources stored in their head, whose exact origin is long forgotten. I am greatly indebted to the tradition of worship, both Anglican and Roman Catholic, in which I have been brought up. Over many years I must have absorbed phrases and images that I cannot now attribute. So should any reader recognize here words, phrases, expressions or patterns of speech that are their own, I would hope that they would understand the difficulty of seeking permission to reproduce what is unconsciously quoted, and also the fact that such unconscious borrowing is a tribute to their work.

If any copyright material is found here which has been used without permission or acknowledgement, this is solely due to my own inadvertence. I, or the publishers, shall be grateful to be informed. The necessary attribution will be included in any future editions.

The Scripture-related opening prayers are original compositions. Many of the other prayers, including the prefaces, are translations or adaptations of texts in the *Missale Romanum* and *Missale Ambrosianum* the Roman and Ambrosian (Milanese) missals. Where I have used prefaces from the *Missale Ambrosianum*, these are taken from the versions published in

Sources and Acknowledgements

We Give You Thanks and Praise – The Ambrosian Eucharistic Prefaces (Canterbury Press 1999).

All Gospel Acclamations are taken from The New Revised Standard Version of the Bible (Anglicized Edition) © 1989, 1995 by the Division of the National Council of Churches of Christ in the United States of America and are used by permission. All rights reserved.

Here are details of the hymn books cited in the text:

The New English Hymnal, Canterbury Press, Norwich 1986.

Laudate, a Hymn Book for the Liturgy, Decani Music, Mildenhall 1999.

Chants De Taizé 2002–2003, Ateliers et Presses De Taizé, 71250 Taizé Communauté, France. (Collections of Taizé chants also exist in many English publications.)

Enemy of Apathy, by John Bell and Graham Maule with the Wild Goose Worship Group, Iona Community 1988.

Hymns for Today's Church, Hodder and Stoughton 1982.